Women of War: Selected Memoirs, Poems, and Fiction by Virginia Women Who Lived Through the Civil War

EDITED BY CASEY CLABOUGH

Texas Review Press
Huntsville, Texas

FIRST EDITION

Requests for permission to acknowledge material from this work should be sent to:

Permissions
Texas Review Press
English Department
Sam Houston State University
Huntsville, TX 77341-2146

Acknowledgements

Several contemporary Virginia women contributed to the assembly of this collection. Julie Allen, Katelyn Carey, and Julie Williams all aided me in the various tasks of technology matters and editing. I also am grateful for the assistance of the staffs at the following scholarly holdings sites: Library of Virginia, University of North Carolina, University of Virginia, and Virginia Historical Society.

Library of Congress Cataloging-in-Publication Data

Women of war (2014)
  Women of war : selected memoirs, poems, and fiction by Virginia women who lived through the Civil War / edited by Casey Clabough. — First edition.
    pages cm
  ISBN 978-1-937875-49-7 (pbk. : alk. paper)
  1. American literature — Women authors. 2. American literature — 19th century. 3. American literature — Virginia. 4. United States — History — Civil War, 1861-1865 — Literary collections. 5. United States — History — Civil War, 1861-1865 — Personal narratives, Confederate. 6. United States — History — Civil War, 1861-1865 — Women. 7. Virginia — Biography. I. Clabough, Casey, 1974 — editor of compilation. II. Title.

  PS508.W7W595 2014
  810.8'0928709755 — dc23
                              2013039500

For the Women

Contents

FICTION

The mission of woman: permitted to bruise
The head of the serpent, and sweetly infuse,
Through the sorrow and sin of earth's registered curse,
The blessing which mitigates all: born to nurse
And to soothe and to solace, to help and to heal
The sick world that leans on her.

— Epigraph to Mary Tucker Magill's
Woman, Or Chronicles of the Late War

But to understand what happened to the South's soul during those four terrible years, we must know what happened to her body, that central battlefield of the war.

— Virginia Moore

Foreword

When my fourth-grade teacher at Glen Allen Elementary School learned that an author of children's books lived in Richmond, just nine miles away, she hatched a plan. The writer was Helen Monsell, who had produced more than twenty volumes, including biographies of Thomas Jefferson, Susan B. Anthony, and Robert E. Lee. Her books were on the shelves of the school's tiny library, and I had read them.

It was Spring, 1968.

My teacher was the popular Elsie Mae Ball. She took me aside and said, "Cary, if I invite Miss Monsell to visit our class, do you think your mother could bring her here?" She wrote a note addressed to "Mrs. George Holladay" and sent it home with me.

My mother had majored in English at William and Mary. She read the note and thought about it. The responsibility of driving a stranger made her nervous, but she wanted to help. She agreed on the condition that I be allowed to go, too. Mrs. Ball gave permission, and soon it was arranged. I was delighted to have Mama all to myself for a trip into Richmond during school hours.

"I would have been scared to have her in the car, alone," Mama admitted as we drove through sunlit streets, past front yards spilling over with pink azaleas. She found the neighborhood, a lovely one not too far from Kensington Avenue, where she had grown up and where her mother, my beloved grandmother "Gee-Gee," still lived. Girlish and exuberant, Gee-Gee had already been apprised of the day's plan. We were to call her later and let her know how it went.

We rang the bell of a stately townhouse, and a woman with beautiful white hair appeared. Mama drove us to the school, where Helen Monsell addressed the class. I was too excited, too awash in vicarious glory, to take in anything she said. My classmates were captivated by our celebrity: she was a hit.

Afterward, when Mama and I took her home, she gave me a present, a typewritten page from the original manuscript of her biography of Dolly Madison, and said good-bye.

Having safely delivered our guest, Mama leaned over the steering wheel and heaved a great sigh. There had been no accident with the Famous Author, no getting lost, nothing horrible happening, the whole event a success by anybody's reckoning. On the way back to school, Mama was giddy with relief. I read the page about Dolly Madison over and over.

I still have it.

Helen Monsell's work doesn't appear in this volume. She was born in 1895, a couple of generations later than these writers, but she was a living connection to them. Growing up, she must have heard first-hand accounts of the Civil War. Though I never saw her again, she was an influence on me, a Virginia woman who wrote.

I understood how divisive that war had been, if only because of a comment attributed to my late great-grandfather, a Virginia farmer who served as a quartermaster under Jubal Early. Of a son's marriage to a Philadelphia debutante, in 1907, the old quartermaster said, "It was too soon," meaning, to take a Yankee bride. The remark was whispered down through generations. It must have reached the ears of the bride, who by the 1960's was my imposing paternal grandmother, a skilled horsewoman who presided over the Orange County farm like an empress, having outlived her husband and her disapproving father-in-law. Though she had resided in Virginia for more than sixty years, she was still an anomaly, a quintessential Yankee—brusque, powerful, and triumphant. She liked horses and dogs better than people, and said so.

The writers in this anthology shared a consciousness of the profound transformation of their world, which we see in the theme of epiphany that runs through these selections. As Mary Spear Tiernan writes, "Feelings in times of high pressure, like flowers forced in artificial temperature, are of quick birth . . . ." Women whose lives would likely have mirrored their mothers' were thrust into catastrophe. Endangered and often impoverished, they wrote diaries, memoirs, poetry, and novels in response to the war that rocked their patriarchal society.

With their men gone, they may have felt some degree of liberation. No matter how much injury the war wreaked upon them, it also provided an opportunity for literary development in those with the ability and inclination to write about dramatic events.

Casey Clabough has created a remarkable volume. I had encountered the work of Sara Rice Pryor and Judith Brockenbrough McGuire in previous anthologies, but Clabough's book is entirely new in its focus on Virginia women who experienced and wrote about the Civil War. Keenly aware of themselves as female, Southern, and Virginian, they were finding new dimensions of identity, recording events that resonated beyond the personal. Yet the individual response, the idiosyncratic detail, gives these excerpts their strength.

War widened their sphere beyond family, neighbors, and friends to include populations they wouldn't otherwise have encountered. Mary Lockett

Avary observes that bereaved women actually "died of grief" after the Battle of Seven Pines. Mary Tucker Magill describes citizens' responses to the Battle of Kernstown, near Winchester: "Every house-top was covered with anxious listeners in various attitudes, expressive of their overwhelming agony of suspense." Thus did these writers (and other women, who didn't write or whose work has been lost) become part of a larger, imperiled community.

Their experiences offer a sharp, convincing savor. The nonfiction sections in particular show initiative, resourcefulness, and crisp observation. Concerned about Winchester's barefoot nurses, Magill asks Stonewall Jackson for the services of a shoemaker. He complies, and soon the nurses have footwear. Volunteering at a hospital, Pryor faints at the sight of a " . . . red stump of an amputated arm." Rallying, she works twelve-hour shifts amid a "harvest of wounded" and "the sickening, dead odor in the hospital, mingled with that of acids and disinfectants." Sallie Brock Putnam vividly evokes the evacuation of Richmond. Confederate soldiers burned warehouses and blew up gunboats to prevent use by the enemy. The blasts shattered windows two miles away. Putnam depicts an entire city on fire, "the roaring . . . heard above the shouting," and "the immense crowd of plunderers . . . moving amid the dense smoke like demons . . . ." Swept along by history, she fought back by reporting it.

These were women of means and privilege, educated or self-educated, many of them slaveholders and all, so far as is known, white. They acknowledge the contributions of enslaved servants — Pryor notes a man named John who forages to feed the household; McGuire quotes an aunt whose "two faithful servants, Jacob and Anthony, kept watch . . . " as federals approached — without once examining the morality of chattel slavery. Discussion of this or other immediate or proximate causes of the war is absent, as is any mention of sex. Yet bloodlust registers here. McGuire records with satisfaction the deaths of Federal troops in "Grant's Mine," meaning the Crater at the Battle of Petersburg.

Daily privation nipped painfully: a spool of cotton cost $5. Rye coffee and sassafras tea made poor substitutes for better beverages. Yet inconvenience was one thing, horror quite another. Avary shares a hotel room with a friend whose satchel holds the bones of a freshly dead son who was unsuccessfully operated upon.

In an era when a linen cabinet indicated a person's status, Pryor donated a vast collection of draperies and tablecloths to the hospital: "My springlike green and white chintz bandages appeared on many a manly arm and leg." In a memorable glimpse, her gaze follows a corpse-laden wagon: "In it a stiff arm was raised, and shook as it was driven down the street . . . ."

The poetry in this volume is notable for the fact that war was previously an uncommon subject for those few American females who wrote poetry at all. Gladly I make the acquaintance of Susan Archer Tally, Fannie H. Marr, and other poets.

Likewise, the fiction selections bring unknown novelists out of the shadows. Marion Harland's *Sunnybank* offers a scene of dramatic tension. Women on their porch are accosted by federal troops demanding food. The narrator's father is a Union sympathizer whose two sons joined the rebel army. The reader is reminded of Virginia's fractured allegiances.

Passages of *Jack Horner* by Mary Spear Tiernan show admirable originality. The protagonist is ever conscious of soldiers' tramping feet, " . . . this tread of a voiceless, never ending army which followed into her dreams . . . ."

Emma Lyon Bryan's *1860-1865: A Romance of the Valley* includes a passage about Southern soldiers knocking at the front door of a house, whereas Northern troops rapped on the back, a detail that probably bespeaks a little-known social reality.

Thanks to Clabough, these writers emerge from obscurity to be read in a future distant from them by a hundred and fifty years. An old Gaelic proverb says, "If you want an audience, start a fight." This book reveals individual females in the war's vast citizen audience. Thanks to McGuire, for example, we learn that a friend felt " . . . as if she were nightly encircled by fire — camp-fires, picket-fires, with here and there stacks of wheat burning . . . ." As these women gave voice to the turbulence in their lives, their words were imbued with courage, and their stakes rose higher. By writing, each claimed her own place in an exploding world.

Their Virginia became mine, though I can only imagine how it might have felt to belong to a separate country. As a child, I dug arrowheads out of Henrico County clay, my imagination fired by stories of Chickahominys who had hunted on land where I climbed trees and helped my mother hang the wash on a clothesline. On a field trip to the Museum of the Confederacy, I was enthralled by hard tack: hundred-year-old food.

By the late 1960's, my elementary school was integrated by a single African-American child in each classroom. If they were scared or reluctant, they didn't let it show. When the teacher led the class in singing "The Erie Canal," "Supper on the Grass," "Bring Me Little Water, Sylvie," and "Dixie," they sang too.

All around us were remnants of earlier times. Glen Allen's landmark was a huge hotel, built in the 1880's by a former Confederate sharpshooter. Decades of disrepair had turned it into a rural tenement with pigeons winging through empty windows. I thought it was beautiful, and it inspired in me a love of things that were vanishing.

I understood that the massive bronze figures

along Richmond's Monument Avenue showed reverence for men who had fought and lost a bitter conflict. My parents were Virginians. They loved the Old Dominion, yet they believed the North's victory was right and inevitable. As we drove past those statues on summer evenings, the air sweet with boxwood and loud with cicadas, my heart lifted. The street's beauty was somber. My mother, born in 1925, had seen Confederate veterans with her own green eyes. "They'd be out on the porch of the soldiers' home," she said. "They were real old. And then they were gone." Her elderly Tidewater relatives still said "gyarden" for "garden." When we visited my father's family in Rapidan, the air smelled of wood smoke, and the rugged hills and sloping pastures appeared unchanged from 19th-century photographs.

It seemed to me that World War II and Vietnam belonged to everybody, but the Civil War belonged to the South and to Virginia most of all. Early on, I grasped the notions of paradox and contra-diction. Virginia's social culture was slow to change. Women's worlds were home, garden club, tea room. Women whispered, smiled, and communicated through innuendo and understatement. My mother's shy, expressive face conveyed emotions she never put into words — emotions for which words don't even exist. The school principal would call her for advice: he knew she didn't gossip.

"Write, Cary," Mama urged me, her voice filled with a sense of mission that felt burdensome to me when I was a teenager and churning out a newspaper column about school activities, dutifully sanitized for the public.

My mother had graduated from college at a time when comparatively few women did so. She knew that publication was as potent an equalizer as the vote. In middle age, she wrote regularly, and her work flourished. Her stories for children appeared in journals. For years, she wrote an antiques column for the Culpeper Star-Exponent. She also wrote literary fiction, unusual stories shared only with relatives. Most of my fiction concerns Southern women, or Northern females in a Southern setting, a fact that has everything to do with the women in my family, especially my mother.

The authors in this book endured in a Virginia that by war's end was permanently altered. Clabough's biographical notes give context to lives that often extended for decades beyond Appomattox. Mary Tucker Magill wrote to support herself. Cornelia Jordan's books were burned by Reconstruction authorities who found the Lynchburg poet's work subversive. Prolific Marion Harland lived more than ninety years. Sara Pryor, who was in her thirties during the war, produced all five of her books after age seventy.

For me, it is Pryor's bell-clear voice that resonates most. Trying to fall asleep in Richmond on the eve of battle, the terrified Pryor, a native of Halifax County, recalls a long-ago night in childhood when she came to Richmond from the country and heard a watchman cry, "'All's well!' Presently the cry was repeated at a distance—'All's well!' Fainter and fainter grew the echo until it became a whisper, far away in the distant streets." Thus are two vanished epochs folded into one tantalizing passage.

By giving twenty-first century recognition to these writers, Casey Clabough also pays tribute to Virginia women now alive. Whether or not we share these authors' sensibilities, we can appreciate the reclamation of those who wrote what they knew when life was hard.

—*Cary Holladay*
Rapidan, Virginia

Introduction

In their variety, the memoir, poetry, and fiction included in this collection show the transitory nature of the literature of southern women who lived through an extraordinarily violent and defining crossroads in their lives. In rare and rediscovered prose and verse excerpts, these women writers evidence the early hopes of a war destined to be lost, the propagandic rhetoric which accompanied it, and the physical and psychological destruction ultimately visited upon them, their homes, and their families. Paradoxically, even as these women defended and spoke out for a cause concerned in part with extending human bondage, they found themselves forced, ready or not, to experience the harsh wind of unprecedented freedom and personal agency as their husbands, sons, and fathers abandoned them and, in many cases, never returned. Writing was one of the new doors opened to them, though the agonizing subject was the death of loved ones and the destruction of their civilization. Indeed, many women wrote with the self-imposed burden and urgency that their narratives, should they escape destruction, might well constitute the only records of their state's struggle.

The selections in this account all arrive from published writings, which means the authors actively sought audiences for their writing: readers specifically interested in southern women's accounts standing in contrast to interpretations of the war by northern historians and southern male writers. As will appear evident over the course of the book, the memoir accounts were focused primarily on the personal privations of women on the home front during the war, while much of the poetry and fiction were penned for propagandic purposes—as rallying calls in the midst of the struggle or political and moral justifications in its wake. While much of the writing herein, including the nonfiction, will appear romantic and sentimental by current literary standards, it should be remembered the authors merely were writing under the conventions of their times. Indeed, there exist narratives by male veterans—one thinks of some of the works of John Esten Cooke, for example—which indulge in romance to a greater degree than most of the pieces in this collection. Though narratives of the war by southern male veterans outnumber those of women authors, the volume of female writing is significant enough to have helped shape what the war and its loss meant to the South as a whole.

Of the women included here, much or little may be related in the contributor's section, depending on the individual writer and her particular circumstances. The memoir section opens with an offering from Mary Tucker Magill, who in addition to writing about her experiences during the war, also authored textbooks on southern history, served as an early advocate of exercise for women, and became known as a distinguished educator. At the far extreme of Magill's notable biography are the poems in the collection which appear either anonymously or under pen names. While authors like Magill—who descended from a distinguished family and whose father was a professor at the University of Virginia—experienced little or no self-consciousness or other barriers writing as women, others were less comfortable or fortunate and so hid their identities beneath faux identities or chose not to employ names at all.

The pieces in this collection have been chosen

carefully, organized by genre, and arranged chrono-logically (either in terms of publication dates or events occurring during the war) or thematically, as seems most appropriate. A book that should prove useful to literary scholars, historians, and anyone possessed of an interest in the Civil War, *Women of War* brings together and to light a cornucopia of heretofore forgotten or obscure women's writings which enrich our understanding of a complex, unsettling time unmatched in our nation's history.

—*Casey Clabough*
Appomattox, Virginia

MEMOIRS

Introduction

From *Woman, or a Chronicle of the late War* (1867)

Mary Tucker Magill

A TRUE artist, before he touches his canvas, paints upon the retina of his mind's eye a perfect representation of the scene he wishes to portray with the skilful pencil of his fancy here deepening a shade and there developing an expression, until he sees it the perfect embodiment of his idea; nor does he rest satisfied until the glowing canvas presents a reflection of this, its original.

A true orator, whose office it is to deal with the passions of the multitude, to sway and control them at his will by his use of language gesture and eye, before he can accomplish his end must bear upon his own heart the impress of the feeling he describes. Language the most beautiful falls powerless unless the heart be in it, while the most thrilling eloquence is the eloquence of deep feeling.

The author combines these two arts, merges them into one. He too paints his scenes upon the retina of his mind's eye and reflects them in language. He too is obliged to bear upon his heart the impress of the feeling he would describe, and that also with a vividness and power equal to if not exceeding that which he would excite; and so it must be that the author suffers keenly in portraying human passion and Buffering, because he must in every case make it his own.

This being the case, it cannot be wondered at that

the task just accomplished in these pages has been a painful one; and the more so that each incident, if not real, had its counterpart in the author's own experience or that of her friends. It has been the waking of the echoes of old trials, the evoking from the chambers of memory scenes which had just fallen into their first slumber there: the tender smile of recollection, which itself has a tear in it, of old laughter and happiness, not the less intense because they came as the reaction of the heart from anxiety and grief, the summoning from their graves friends dead and gone, and making them live and act once more on the mimic stage of her fancy. Often has the pen faltered and her heart grown faint over her task; but with *nature* as her inspiration and *truth* as her guide, she has persevered to the end. How the work has been accomplished, she leaves it to the judgment of the public to decide — a public which has proved so kind to her in the past that she dares regard it as her friend.

The theme chosen is no uncommon one, perhaps, though in the treatment given, it can scarce be regarded as hackneyed. It is more the fashion to lay the scenes of a war story on the battle-field, in the camp and the toilsome march, to write of deeds dared by these whose province it is to act the more vigorous part in such scenes. But this is a story of WOMAN in her proper sphere, by the fireside, in her household duties, and by the side of the sick and dying. It is a simple, unexaggerated narrative of what non-combatants are forced to endure in a country torn by intensive strife, and for its truth I appeal not only to my own country-women, but to the world; and I hear an echo from the mountains of Switzerland and the fair plains of Italy, while Poland and Greece take up the refrain, and France, baring her breast all gory with recent wounds, cries aloud for a pen of fire with which to write her story.

The title of the book was first suggested by an incident in which the author was an actor. Its narration may not be without interest. It was in November of 1862, after the bloody battle of Antietam, when the town of Winchester constituted the field-hospital for the army. Every building devoted to such purposes was crowded; the private houses also were filled, and even along the streets the sufferers lay, affording a moving spectacle of the horrors of war.

The rapid transitions of the army had rendered it impossible to supply the sick and wounded with such comforts as they needed. A pallet of straw and coarse army fare was the lot of all, no matter what their condition and rank.

In this state of affairs it may be inferred that the ladies of the town were not, backward in their efforts to supply, so far as their means allowed, what was lacking; and when their resources were exhausted they still gave their time and services. Night and day found them in attendance on the poor sufferers. They did not hesitate to take the hospitals under their care even, and with all their energies strove to ameliorate the sufferings which met them at every turn.

But an obstacle occurred which threatened to be serious, if not insurmountable. In the decimation of all the callings of trade which the war occasioned, there was not a shoemaker in the town, out of the army, and the ladies were seriously embarrassed by the fact that their shoes were completely worn out, not even affording sufficient protection to enable them to pursue their walks to the hospitals with comfort.

In this emergency it was suggested that if an application were made, it would be an easy matter to have a shoemaker detailed from the ranks who would in a short time remedy the problem.

Acting upon this, the author of these pages, as the representative of her companions, made the application to General Jackson himself, by letter, in which she took the ground that although nature and custom combined to exclude women from a more active participation in scenes of warfare, yet were they, in pursuing their walks among the sick and suffering, in relieving the wants of the destitute, as truly the soldiers of the South as the men, and as such their *absolute wants* should be supplied. A statement of these was then made, and the request preferred that Sergeant Faulkner, a young tradesman of the town, might be detailed to make shoes for the ladies who attended the hospitals.

In writing a story of the "Lost Cause," the author has fully appreciated the delicacy and difficulty of the task. Acknowledging the expediency of "seeking those things which make for peace," she has earnestly desired to avoid the bitterness and recrimination which formed so prominent a feature in the domestic scenes of the war. She has attempted no political view of the subject; she has never once attacked the actions of the Government; she has simply amplified the fact that there are bad men and tyrants in every army, who will not hesitate to use the power entrusted to them for military purposes, merely to serve their own ends or gratify a private grievance, and hence a great deal of the suffering which is inseparable from a state of war.

For the Cause itself she has only to say that History, which seldom espouses the cause of the vanquished, may bring in a verdict of guilty against it, may decide that the sacrifices made and the terrible agonies endured were in the cause of wrong and oppression; but if ever there was pure patriotism, an earnest, honest conviction of right, it nerved the arms and inspired the hearts of the people of the South. And for the women: as a mother clasps in her loving embrace her new-born child, and rejoices in its perfection of life and limb and that it is all her own, so did they love the "Cause" in its new birth; and when the blood began to flow, and they looked upon its fair young face all marred and bleared by its suffering, they but hugged it the closer to their breasts; and when at last they laid it a dead corpse under the sods of Appomattox, they wept bitter tears over its place. And still with pious sorrow do they trace out its footsteps through the length and breadth of the land, remembering them of each trait which endeared it to them; laughing and weeping in a breath as recollection brings back its scenes of sorrow and triumph, of joy and humiliation; and through it all, turning aside from a contemplation of secondary causes, they bow beneath the hand which dealt the blow, saying, "It is the Lord: let Him do as seemeth Him good."

Chapter IV: The Realities of War

From A Virginia Girl in the Civil War (1903)

Mary Lockett Avary

WHEN Dan recovered I returned to Norfolk, and there I stayed for some time, getting letters from him, taking care of uncle and developing a genius for housekeeping. One day I was out shopping when I saw everybody running toward the quay. I turned and went with the crowd. We saw the Merrimac swing out of the harbor—or did she crawl? A curious looking craft she was, that first of our ironclads, ugly and ominous.

She had not been gone many hours when the sound of guns came over the water followed by silence, terrible silence, that lasted until after the lamps were lit. Suddenly there was tumultuous cheering from the quay. The Merrimac had come home after destroying the Cumberland and the Congress.

"Well for the Congress!" we said. Her commander had eaten and drunk of Norfolk's hospitality, and then had turned his guns upon her—upon a city full of his friends. Bravely done, Merrimac! But that night I cried myself to sleep. Under the sullen waters of Hampton Roads slept brave men and true, to whom Stars and Stripes and Southern Cross alike meant nothing now. The commander of the Congress was among the dead, and he had been my friend—I had danced with him in my father's house. Next day, the Monitor met the Merrimac and turned the tide of victory against us.

Her commander was John L. Worden, who had been our guest beloved.

During all this time I had been separated from my husband. He had been detailed to make a survey of Pig Point and the surrounding country, and it was not until he reached Smithfield that he sent for me. We were beginning now to realize that war was upon us in earnest. There was the retreat from Yorktown; Norfolk was evacuated troops were moving. Everything was bustle and confusion. My husband went off with his command, the order for departure so sudden that he had not time to plan for me.

As Northern troops began to occupy the country, fearing that I would be left in the enemy's lines and so cut off from getting to him, I took the matter into my own hands and went in a covered wagon to Zuni, twenty miles distant, where I had heard that his command was encamped for a few days. After a rough ride I got there only to find that my husband had started off to Smithfield for me. We had passed each other on the road, each in a covered wagon. There was nothing to do except to wait his return that night.

As my husband's command had been ordered to join the troops at Seven Pines, I took the train for Richmond the next day, stopped a few hours, and then went to Petersburg. When I got there the Battle of Seven Pines was on. For two days it raged — for two days the booming of the cannon sounded in our ears and thundered at our hearts. Friends gathered at each other's houses and looked into each other's faces and held each other's hands, and listened for news from the field. And the sullen boom of the cannon broke in upon us, and we would start and shiver as if it had shot us, and sometimes the tears would come. But the bravest of us got so we could not weep. We only sat in silence or spoke in low voices to each other and rolled bandages and picked linen into lint. And in those two days it seemed as if we forgot how to smile.

Telegrams began to come; a woman would drop

limp and white into the arms of a friend — her husband was shot. Another would sit with her hand on her heart in pallid silence until her friends, crowding around her, spoke to her, tried to arouse her, and then she would break into a cry:

"O my son! my son!"

There were some who could never be roused any more; grief had stunned and stupefied them forever, and a few there were who died of grief. One young wife, who had just lost her baby and whose husband perished in the fight, never lifted her head from her pillow. When the funeral train brought him home we laid her in old Blandford beside him, the little baby between.

Now and then when mothers and sisters were bewailing their loss and we were pressing comfort upon them, there would be a whisper, and one of us would turn to where some poor girl sat, dumb and stricken, the secret of her love for the slain wrenched from her by the hand of war. Sometimes a bereaved one would laugh!

The third day, the day after the battle, I heard that Dan was safe. Every day I had searched the columns of "Killed and Wounded" in the *Richmond Dispatch* for his name, and had thanked God when I didn't find it. But direct news I had none until that third day. The strain had been too great; I fell ill. Owing to the general's illness at this time his staff was ordered to Petersburg, and Dan, who was engineer upon the staff, got leave to come on for a day or two in advance of the other members of it; but while I was still at death's door he was ordered off. When I at last got up, I had to be taught to walk as a child is taught, step by step; and before I was able to join my husband many battles had been fought in which he took part. I was at the breakfast-table, when, after months of weary waiting, he telegraphed me to come to Culpeper Courthouse.

This time I packed a small trunk with necessary

articles, putting in heavy dresses and winter flannels. The winter does not come early in Petersburg; the weather was warm when I started, and I decided to travel in a rather light dress for the season. I did not trouble myself with hand-baggage not even a shawl. The afternoon train would put me in Richmond before night; I would stop over until morning, and that day's train would leave me in Culpeper. Just before I started, Mr. Sampson, at whose house I was staying, came in and said that an old friend of his was going to Richmond on my train and would be glad to look after me. I assented with alacrity.

Before the war it was not the custom for ladies to travel alone, and, besides this, in the days of which I write traveling was attended with much confusion and many delays. I reached the depot a few minutes before train time, my escort was presented and immediately took charge of me. He was a nice looking elderly gentleman, quite agreeable, and with just a slight odor of brandy about him. He saw me comfortably seated, and went to see after our baggage, he said. He did not return at once, but I took it for granted that he was in the smoking-car. Traveling was slower then than now. Half-way to Richmond I began to wonder what had become of my escort. But my head was too full of other things to bother very much about it. The outlook from the car window along that route is always beautiful; and then, the next day I was to see Dan. Darkness, and across the river the lights of Richmond flashed upon the view. Where was my escort? I had noticed on the train that morning a gentleman who wore the uniform of a Confederate captain and whom I knew by sight. He came up to me now.

"Excuse me, madam, but can I be of any assistance to you? I know your husband quite well."

"Do you know where my escort is?" I asked.

He looked embarrassed and tried not to smile.

"We left him at Chester, Mrs. Grey."

"At Chester? He was going to Richmond."

"Well—you see, Mrs. Grey, it was—an accident. The old gentleman got off to get a drink and the train left him."

I could not help laughing. "If you will allow me, madam," said my new friend, "I will see you to your hotel. How about your baggage?"

"Oh!" I cried in dismay, "Mr. C has my trunk-check in his pocket."

My new friend considered. "If he comes on the next train, perhaps that will be in time to get your trunk off with you to Culpeper, if not, your trunk will follow you immediately. I'll see the conductor and do what I can. I'm going out of town tomorrow, but Captain Jeter is here and I'll tell him about your trunkcheck. He'll be sure to see Mr. C."

I was to see Dan the next day, and nothing else mattered. I made my mind easy about that trunk, and my new friend took me to the American, where I spent the evening very pleasantly in receiving old acquaintances and making new ones.

But with bedtime another difficulty arose: I had never slept in a room at a hotel by myself in my life. Fortunately, Mrs. Hopson, of Norfolk, happened to be spending the night there. I sent up a note asking if I might sleep with her, and went up to her room half an hour later prepared for a delightful talk about Norfolk. When we were ready for bed, she took up one of her numerous satchels and put it down on the side where I afterward lay down to sleep.

"I put that close by the bed because it contains valuables," she said with an impressive solemnity I afterward understood.

Of course I asked no questions, though she referred to the valuables several times. We were in bed and the lights had been out some time when I had occasion to ask her where she had come from there.

"Oh, Nell" she said, "didn't you know? I've been to Charlottesville and I've come from there today. Didn't you know about it? John" (her son) "was wounded. Didn't you know about it? Of course I had to go to him. They had to perform an operation on him. I was right there when they did it."

Here followed a graphic account of the operation. "It was dreadful, You see that satchel over there?" pointing to the one just beneath my head on the floor.

"Yes, I see it."

"Well, John's bones are right in there!"

"Good gracious!" I cried, and jumped over her to the other side of the bed.

"Why, what's the matter?" she asked. "You look like you were scared, Nell. Why, Nell, the whole of John wouldn't hurt you, much less those few bones. I'm carrying them home to put them in the family burying ground, That's the reason I think so much of that satchel and keep it so close to me. I don't want John to be buried all about in different places, you see. But I don't see anything for you to be afraid of in a few bones. John's as well as ever — it isn't like he was dead, now."

I lay down quietly, ashamed of my sudden fright, but there were cold chills running down my spine.

After a little more talk she turned over, and I presently heard a comfortable snore, but I lay awake a long time, my eyes riveted on the satchel containing fragments of John. Then I began to think of seeing Dan in the morning, and fell asleep feeling how good it was that he was safe and sound, all his bones together and not scattered around like poor John's.

I reached Culpeper Courthouse the next afternoon about four o'clock. Dan met me looking tired and shabby, and as soon as he had me settled went back to camp.

"I'll come to see you as often as I can get leave," he said when he told me goodby. "We may be quartered here for some time — long enough for us to get ourselves and our horses rested up, I hope; but I'm afraid I can't see much of you. Hardly worth the trouble of your coming, is it, little woman?"

"Oh, Dan, yes," I said cheerfully; "just so you are not shot up! It would be worth the coming if I only got to see you through a car window as the train went by."

A few days after my arrival a heavy snow storm set in. As my trunk had not yet come, I was still in the same dress in which I had left Petersburg, and, though we were all willing enough to lend, clothes were so scarce, that borrowing from your neighbor was a last resort. I suffered in silence for a week before my trunk arrived, and then it was exchanging one discomfort for another, for my flannels were so tight from shrinkage and so worn that I felt as if something would break every time I moved.

During this snow-storm the roads were lined with Confederate troops marching home footsore and weary from Maryland. Long, hard marches and bloody battles had been their portion. In August they had come, after their work at Seven Pines, Cold Harbor, and Malvern Hill, to drive Pope out of Culpeper, where he was plundering. They had driven him out and pressed after, fighting incessantly. Near Culpeper there had been the battle of Cedar Mountain, where Jackson had defeated Pope and chased him to Culpeper Courthouse. Somewhat farther from Culpeper had been fought the second battle of Manassas, and, crowding upon these, the battles of Gerrmantown, Centreville, Antietam — more than I can remember to name. Lee's army was back in Culpeper now with Federal troops at their heels, and McClellan, not Pope, in command. Civilians, women, children, and slaves feared Pope; soldiers feared McClellan — that is, as much as Lee's soldiers could fear anybody.

I found our tired army in Culpeper trying to rest and fatten a little before meeting McClellan's legions. Then — I am not historian enough to know just how it happened — McClellan's head fell and Burnside reigned in his stead. Better and worse for our army, and no worse for our women and children, for Burnside was a gentleman even as McClellan was and as Pope was not, and made no war upon women and children until the shelling of Fredericksburg.

Chapter XIII: Rebel Strategy Resulting in the Battle of Kernstown

From *Woman, or a Chronicle of the Late War (1867)*

Mary Tucker Magill

"When Greeks joined Greeks, then came the tug of war."

THE position of the Confederate army at Manassas was one of great interest and peril. The United States, profiting by their late lesson, were gathering their forces most vigorously; able officers were appointed to the various commands, and the prosecution of the war was determined upon a far more energetic scale than heretofore. They had underrated the strength and endurance of the Southern troops, but since "Greek met Greek" this was no longer the case, and General Johnston found it necessary to contract his line of defence by drawing the enemy further inward from his supplies, as something towards equalizing the relative strength of the two armies. But to accomplish his task required all of his thought and wariness. Did the Federals once suspect his design, they might precipitate an attack which would not only be fatal to his army, but to the Confederate capital and even to the Southern cause. So the greatest secrecy was maintained about all of his movements; daily the railroad trains were quietly packed with stores, but the constant activity along the lines and apparent preparation for a forward move kept suspicion away.

The large army at Winchester, however, under Shields and Banks, gave General Johnston more disquiet than even the larger one in front of him, because they were really in his rear, and by making a forced march across the mountains, as General Jackson had done prior to the battle of Manassas, they could place him between two powerful armies and inevitably crush him. That this was their intention he had every reason to know; and he had daily reports from Winchester of indications leading to this move. In his dilemma General Johnston sent a dispatch ordering General Jackson, if possible, to engage Banks's army so as to prevent this movement, though he had no men to send to assist in the effort. General Jackson was not a man to look at second causes. He knew the danger to be imminent, and he knew also that his small force was outnumbered three or four times at least by Banks in Winchester, but even under these circumstances he determined to make an attack. Nor did he despair of victory; he knew that there was *One* who could if He pleased give it to him; could make "one chase a thousand, and two put ten thousand to flight." He found when he had turned towards Winchester that there was no time to be lost; the dreaded movement had already commenced. A large portion of the force of General Banks were moving in the direction of Manassas.

Ashby's dash into Winchester, of which we have already given some account, was made to draw out the force from the town in order that they might be able to judge of the numbers they would have opposed to them. It was eminently successful, as the entire Federal force, as if in obedience to his summons, was drawn-out around the town. A slight skirmish took place, in which General Shields, the Federal commandant of the post in conjunction with General Banks, had his right arm broken by a chance shell.

The next morning the battle of Kernstown commenced. It took its name from a small hamlet about four miles from Winchester, around which a considerable part of the battle was fought.

It was probably one of the most desperately and well contested battles of the war. General Jackson always spoke of it as such. The disparity of numbers was fearful, but notwithstanding this fact the field was contended for during the entire day, and the result uncertain.

To describe the anxiety of the people of Winchester would be impossible; they knew that the Stonewall Brigade was engaged, and the Stonewall Brigade included all of the young men from the town and country round. The firing was terrible; the booming of the cannon was so continuous that it sounded like crashing thunder. Nor was the illusion destroyed by a nearer view, as the flashes which preceded the discharges were fearful. But the crackling of the musketry was even a more dreadful sound than the cannonading; it lasted without intermission for hours. Every house-top was covered with anxious listeners in various attitudes, expressive of their overwhelming agony of suspense. This was somewhat alleviated by the evident dismay and apprehension of the Federals, who rode about the streets collecting up the stragglers and hurrying them to the front, and by evening these symptoms increased so much that in the same proportion the spirits of the people revived.

"Our men will certainly be in by to-morrow morning," said Ellen Randolph, entering her mother's room with face flushed with excitement. She hesitated when she found that Mrs. Mason was on her knees, and Mrs. Randolph with her Bible on her knee, each trying to draw their strength and support in the hour of fearful trial from the source of all strength.

"How do you know?" said both ladies, rising at the joyful intelligence.

"Well," said Ellen, "I was at the parlor window just now, with the shutters closed, listening for some news from the passers-by. The porch was full of stragglers, one of whom called out to a cavalryman who dashed up the street: "'What news from the battle-field?' 'News?' he said, riding up to the pavement, 'the news is that every one of you ought to be out on the field. I am ordered to gather up all the men about town, and form them into a company and march them out. The fact is we have been flanked, and if some relief does not come in a very short time we will have to retreat. So come on, every man of you.'" And Ellen danced around the room in great excitement.

"My child," said Mrs. Randolph, "you forgot what suffering may come to us, even with a victory."

Ellen stopped. "Indeed, Mamma," she said, " I forgot everything in the triumph."

Night fell at last, and everything was ominously quiet. None of the inhabitants were allowed to go out of their houses after nightfall, so that there was no possibility of hearing anything, though every one continued full of hope until about nine o'clock, when the sound of the military bands playing "Yankee Doodle" at headquarters fell like a knell upon every heart, and the night was passed in all the agony of suspense. Unable to bear it any longer, at the first dawn of day Ellen Randolph rose and determined to go out and find out something. Issuing from the front door, she could see, to her surprise, figures of her own sex passing and repassing in the distance, and occasionally a blue uniform.

Hastening down the street, she encountered a friend with tear-stained face, wringing her hands as she hastened on.

"What is the matter?" she said breathlessly, as she overtook her.

"Matter?" was the answer, in a hollow tone of despair; "don't you know that Jackson's command has been cut all to pieces, and those who are not killed are taken prisoners. The jail, warehouses, and churches are used as prisons for our dear ones. I am just going to hunt for my three boys. I don't know whether they are dead or prisoners." And she wrung her hands again in the extremity of her misery.

Ellen staggered for an instant under the force of the blow, and then hurried on with her companion.

It was even so; they had entered Winchester, but as prisoners. There were comparatively few deaths, however, as a portion of the command had been surrounded and captured entire.

During the day the streets were thronged with women looking in the different prisons for their friends, seeking information of them from the prisoners.

"Can you tell me anything of John Aylet, of the 2nd Virginia?" asked a poor, anxious-looking mother of some prisoners who stood at the open window of one of the houses used as a prison.

"John Aylot, of the 2nd Virginia? Oh yes, he is somewhere here — wounded, I think."

"Wounded? Where?"

"Not bad, I think, ma'am; but he fought by me, and I saw him fall."

Off hurried the poor woman to resume her search.

"Charlie, Charlie, there you are, thank God!" said another, recognizing a brother. "I have been afraid to ask anybody about you; and to think you can't come out — it does seem too hard."

"Might have been worse, Sue," was the cheerful answer. "I tell you it was an awful fight, and many a fine fellow bit the dust; and then to be whipped after all!"

"You made a brave fight though, against fearful odds. I am proud of it."

"For goodness sake, Sue, get us something to eat. We have had nothing since yesterday morning, and are almost starved."

This intimation was enough, and soon the women hurried from place to place with baskets of provision, which they were allowed to pass in at the windows. It was a relief to be able to serve them, and they considered it a favor that they should be permitted to do so.

Indeed, either from policy, which at this stage of the war dictated an indulgent course to the people, or from a desire to be relieved from the trouble of supplying the wants of their prisoners, no interference was made with the action of the citizens in this matter. They were also allowed to take the wounded home to their houses, that they might nurse them.

"Mr. Dallam! Captain Williams!" exclaimed Ellen Randolph, stopping short upon hearing her name called and recognizing these two gentlemen.

"Even so, Miss Randolph," said the last-named gentleman; "fairly caught and caged."

"What have you got in that basket, Miss Randolph?" said Mr. Dallam. "Something to eat, I hope; for I am actually starved."

Ellen quickly handed the basket up to them, and saw its contents distributed to about a dozen men in the room with them.

"What is the news from Rose Hill?" asked she, as they employed themselves.

"I made a dash there the other day," said Mr. Dallam; "found all well, but rather melancholy at the prospect of parting from Mr. Holcombe, who goes to Richmond in a few days to take a post appointment. Your cousin, Miss Mary, is all right. I looked in vain for the qualities you gave her credit for the other day. I know her better than you do," laughing triumphantly.

"Maybe so," said Ellen; "it is too early to decide that matter. How long are you all to be permitted to stay in town?"

"We leave for Baltimore this afternoon, I think," said Captain Williams. "But we will be exchanged very soon, I expect, as we have the majority of prisoners now, and they are glad to exchange."

"I wish we could be exchanged," said Ellen ruefully.

"Never mind; next time we come I hope we will release you," said Mr. Williams. "We tried hard this time, but they were too many for us."

They were marched to the cars under guard that afternoon, and the last sight of them the ladies had were bright familiar faces looking and smiling at them from the dreary box-cars. Captain Williams managed to whisper to Ellen Randolph before he left;

"If you should see your cousin before I do, say to her that I am here thus and now in fulfillment of my promise to her, to which, God helping me, I will be faithful."

Many times did Ellen ponder this message over, but wanted a key to the mystery involved. It was not until a long, long time afterwards that it was furnished to her.

We know now, what was only known at the time to those who were masters of the situation, that the object which General Jackson proposed to accomplish by this desperate battle was fully attained. Several regiments which had actually started towards Manassas were ordered back to Winchester, and General Johnston fell back to a new line of defence without the loss of a single man or a dollar's worth of property. It was considered one of the most masterly retreats of the war, but must have failed disastrously had it not been for the sacrifices made on the battle-field of Kernstown.

Chapter XXVI: A Southern Woman Thrown on Her Own Resources

From *Woman, or a Chronicle of the Late War* (1867)

Mary Tucker Magill

"O Liberty! Liberty! how many crimes are
committed in thy name."
—MADAME ROLAND

WHEN Ellen Randolph looked down the road in
the direction of Winchester at the rapidly disappearing
cavalcade which had acted as her escort, and then
back again in the opposite direction at the desolate
country, it must be confessed that her woman's heart
quailed a little; but gathering courage on the instant
from the very absence of danger, as well as of relief
she walked on to the next house, which she knew well
as the house of kind friends.

"Why, Ellen Randolph! Where on the earth did
you come from?" said a lady, running from the house
to meet her, followed by a young girl.

Laughing and crying all in a breath, the young
lady gave an account of herself and received a warm
welcome as they accompanied her into the house.

"And why not stay with us until our men come
in?" said Agnes Irvine, a pretty rosebud of a girl, not
yet over the threshold of womanhood, but nearing
the boundary.

"Ah, if I only could!" said Ellen; "but I cannot remain so near the lines. I am like poor Joe in 'Bleak House,' I don't know where I am to go, but I must keep 'moving on' until I can find Papa, and consult with him about myself. I feel almost afraid to meet him too, on account of Mamma; I know he will be so worried. Ah, Agnes, my dear!" turning as she spoke to the young girl, who knelt before her and held her hand, and speaking in half comic, half-serious admonition, "take warning from my experience and never write a letter! See what it has brought me to."

"It has brought you to us," said Ellen Irvine kindly; "we cannot be sorry for that."

"You are very kind," said Ellen, her eyes filling, "but I cannot blind myself to the truth that I have acted foolishly, and the result has been unfortunate, to Mamma, at least."

"Oh well, never mind, it will all come right after a while," said the lady consolingly, while Agnes patted her hand with affectionate sympathy. "I don't believe it will be long before you can return home,"

"In the meantime," said Ellen, "how am I to continue my journey ?"

"How indeed?" said Mrs. Irvine; "our army is sixty miles up the Valley, and I do not suppose there are a dozen horses between this place and that."

"Mamma," said Agnes, "old Mr. Brown, our neighbor, has a horse and cart. I wonder if Miss Nell could not hire them?"

"That old thing!" said Mrs. Ervine, laughing; "I don't believe it would drag her ten miles."

"Then let it drag me five," said Ellen, and I will get some other conveyance. We must not despise 'the day of small things.'"

It proved a fortunate suggestion of Agnes Irvine's, as Mr. Brown, upon being applied to, not only furnished the horse and cart, but refused most positively to take any money for its use.

"Far be it from me, young lady," said the old man, leaning on his stick and shaking his gray head with earnest emphasis, "far be it from me to take a cent of money from a young lady who is put upon by these miserable scoundrels, who ain't ashamed to fight a petticoat. I can't fight, Ma'am, I'm too old for that; but I can lend you my horse and cart to take you as far as Woodstock on your journey, and I'll do it and welcome; and all the pay I wants is for you to hunt up my two boys what is in the 1st Virginia Regiment, and tell them if they wants their father's blessing to fight the Yankees all the harder for this deed they's done."

Nothing remained but to take the old man's offer, which Ellen did with many thanks, and the next morning saw her on her way, with Mrs. Irvine's little son as her driver.

The old horse, so contemptuously spoken of by Mrs. Irvine, proved better than his looks, or perhaps he was inspired by the knowledge of the service he was performing. Certain it is that he stepped out bravely, and carried Ellen the first stage of her journey, about twenty miles, accomplishing the feat in time to allow horse, cart, and boy to return to Newtown that night.

Again was Ellen left alone, standing on the low step leading into a long weather-boarded house, ostentatiously introduced as "The Hotel" by the sign-board which swung and creaked above her head. Nothing could be more utterly bare and desolate than the streets of Woodstock looked to the young girl as she stood gazing after the humble vehicle which had borne her so far on her journey. In its best days the town could not have been styled a pretty little village, and now, though there was a uniformity in the low weather, boarded houses, built close to the road, with only an occasional symptom of green grass obtruding itself upon the sight, from the background it was a uniformity of dimness and dilapidation. A few ragged urchins played about the street, and one old man sat with his chair tilted back against the wall of what had once been a store, judging from the ambitions sign-board which still bore its place at the side of the door announcing "Dr-y-goods, Corn, Potatoes, Shoes, Butter, Oats, Spices, Canned-fruit, Books, Confectionary, Stationery, and Fruits for sale here." But the empty windows and shelves, as seen through the open door, denied all of these facts in the most emphatic manner.

So the old man had plenty of time to rest his feet in the air and wonder what the young lady standing on the hotel steps was crying for, and where she came from, and why those lazy rascals in the house didn't come out to see about her. He was just thinking of rousing them to an attention to their duties, and of gratifying his curiosity at the same time, when a portly old gentleman in linsey-woolsey pants and linen coat made his appearance.

"Won't you walk in, Miss?" said he, rousing her by the sound of his voice from the telegraph of thought she was sending down the road to her home.

"Can I go on from here up the Valley?" said Ellen, feeling an unconquerable aversion to entering the house.

"Well, it ain't no easy matter nowadays, Ma'am, to git about," said the man, a little disappointed at the thought of losing a customer so soon.

"Is there no vehicle I can hire to carry me even a few miles? I must go on, if possible, to-night," said Ellen, earnestly.

"Lord love you, Miss!" answered the man, "people have to walk nowadays. The soldiers don't leave much cattle behind 'em when they goes."

"You mean the Yankees take your horses," said Ellen, disposed to espouse the cause of the Confederacy on this its threshold.

"Both sides takes 'em, Miss, can't say I sees much difference in desire for horseflesh between the two."

"Oh well," said Ellen, woman-like, shifting her position to meet the difficulty, "of course our men have a right to them — indeed they are *obliged* to have them; but the Yankees have no right."

"Oh yes, yes, yes; I s'pose it's all right enough," said the man, by hurried acquiescence putting a period to any further discussion; "but walk in, Miss, and we will see if we can't make you comfortable," and he ushered her into a room which evidently held the rank of drawing-room in the establishment, though, like everything around, it bore the marks of the war in the faded and dingy atmosphere which pervaded it. The colors of the calico covering to the home-made lounge, which stretched itself, uninvitingly, opposite the door, had probably in an early stage of their existence delighted the eye of their successful artisan by their brilliancy and variety, but they were now, alas! Bleared and dingy from long use, and the cover itself pleaded through occasional rents for the privilege of rest, to which its long anti faithful servitude entitled it. The chairs were rather in keeping with the lounge, though there was a promise of comfort in the split-bottom rockers of which the hard and impenetrable lounge gave no hope: a rag carpet adorned the floor, with the help here and there afforded by some remnant of better days in the shape of a three-ply scrap at the door and before the fire-place, about which it can only be said they were doing their best to brighten the aspect of things. But the pride of the room was evidently a huge mahogany sofa, covered with black horse-hair, which wheezed with asthmatic indignation at every invasion of its magnificence, and bristled all over with broken springs, to the detriment of any ambitious aspirant to its throne. A centre-table sat between the windows, covered with the inevitable leather-back photographs and some books, distinguished severally by the gilt titles, "*The Pearl,*" "*The Gem,*" "*Album,*" &c. The walls were adorned with works of art in the shape of landscapes, where the excessive blue of the skies was only exceeded by the excessive blue of the water, and where grass of an impossible green luxuriated and afforded pasture for wooden cattle, of what peculiar species it defied the observer to decide; wooden men and women issued from houses smaller than themselves, and trees waved their rare foliage in the breeze.

Ellen Randolph's loneliness perfectly overcame her here, though she struggled bravely against the tears which would come in spite of her. When her host left her alone, to provide for her entertainment, she threw herself into a chair and sought a diversion in surrounding objects. It was at hand in the leather-backed photograph cases, and she was soon smiling amusedly over a rigid pair who had evidently just embarked upon the sea of matrimony, which they announced to all beholders by it stiff embrace. The next was an old grandmamma, with an uncompromising cap-border; next, a Confederate soldier in gray, and a young lady in blue, with innumerable streamers and a general airy appearance, as if she was out in a strong gale. Ellen was just making the acquaintance of this last, and woman-like, forming a link between the original of it and the Confederate boy, when the original, without streamers, and consequently subdued, made her appearance at the door and announced that the young lady's room was ready for her reception.

"It is scarcely worth while," said Ellen, "for me to take a room, as I must leave at once."

"How?" asked the girl.

"That's the difficulty, I acknowledge," said Ellen, "and one I must try to overcome. Is there no one who has a horse I could hire to take me on to Mount Jackson?"

"Well, Pap he used to have a horse and carriage, but he ain't got none now," said the girl, showing a happy talent for retrospect, though scarce bringing it to bear successfully upon present emergencies; "and Tom, my brother,—his likeness is there," (alas! for Ellen's romance), "he's got a horse too, but he ain't here."

It was very satisfactory to the young lady doubtless to reflect that the family had been and were so well provided with means of locomotion, but Ellen could not quite see how it helped the present case.

"But is there no one in town" she said, "who would hire me a horse? Think if there is no horse about here I could get."

"Well now," said the former owner of the streamers, after contemplating the ceiling for some time, "Uncle Jade Slimons he did have two horses, but—"

"Of course he hasn't them now," said Ellen, her patience quite deserting her at the prospect of another chapter of past joys.

"No, the Yankees tuck 'em both. But he's got a cow, if you could—" and she looked suggestively at Ellen.

"Ride a cow!" said Ellen, laughing. "Anxious as I am to get on, I hardly think I could do that,"

"Well, she's dry, en' she's very gentle. I thought maybe you could."

In her desperation, it might have been that even the offer of the cow would have been accepted, but fortunately a diversion was effected by a rolling of wheels, and a lumbering road-wagon, drawn by two meagre horses, which doubtless possessed all the qualifications necessary to private life, and were lame, halt, and blind all three. The wagon was loaded with rather a heterogeneous mingling of fence-rails, timbers with the nails still in them, and gnarled logs of wood, all piled in pell-mell. It was evidently the gleanings of fuel from a deserted camp-ground. But Ellen only saw a way out of her dilemma, and the vehicle had hardly come in sight before she was at the door, hailing the driver. Of course he was old (for but few young men were to be seen outside of the army), and both deaf and blind, as was evident from his obtuseness both to the loud cries of "Stop! Stop!" and the sight of the young lady waving her hand from the doorway. Agonised at the thought of losing an opportunity, our young heroine sped forward like an arrow from the bow, and the driver was almost thrown from his seat by her sudden appearance at his horses' heads. The horses were stopped and the explanation given, though it had to be repeated many times before it reached the ears of the old man.

"And won't you take me on as far as you go?" said Ellen.

The man looked ruefully at the wagon and then at his miserable team.

Ellen understood him without words.

"I don't care how rough it is," she said, approaching him and speaking loud enough even for him to hear without difficulty, "and I am very little weight, indeed I am, and I can walk whenever the horses get tired; but I am so anxious to get on into the Confederate lines. I'll pay you well for your trouble."

"Oh, never mind that," said the old man. "I was jest thinking that it was a pretty rough place for sich a young lady as you; but if you choose to try it to Mount Jackson, you are heartily welcome."

"God bless you for it!" said Ellen, joyfully; "I won't keep you waiting a moment," and in a very short time after she was mounted on her rough seat with her trunk beside her, taking a smiling leave of her quondam host and his daughter, who stood in the road to see her off.

She had scarce calculated her ability to stand the roughness of her vehicle, as it jolted from side to side, bringing her in contact with the timbers most uncomfortably, and in the first half-mile she felt so bruised and sore that she doubted her ability to endure it any longer; but the old man turned round just then to see how she was getting on, a sudden fear of being left behind expanded her face into a smile, and prompted the assurance, delivered with a good deal of courage but very little truth, that she was "getting on delightfully."

And so the process of reducing the young lady to mincemeat continued, she enduring with the greatest fortitude blows which in ordinary times would have brought a shriek to her lips. She could not bear it longer, however, as she felt herself growing faint under the continued suffering.

"How much farther is it to Mount Jackson" she shouted into her companion's ear the next time he turned around towards her.

"What you say?" answered the old man, putting his hand up to his ear and stopping the progress of the wagon.

"How much farther is it to Mount Jackson?" repeated Ellen, in still louder tones.

"No, that ain't Mount Jackson," said he, still obtuse.

"Mount Jackson's a good five mile *furder* yet."

"I believe then I'll have to try and walk it," said Ellen, the tears coming into her eyes as her bruised limbs made themselves evident from sudden change of position.

"Why, what's the matter?" said her guide; "too rough for you?"

"I believe so. I don't think I can stand this any longer; I am suffering so terribly from these boards and logs."

"Hum," grunted the old man, hearing only a portion of her complaint, "ef you can't stand, how do you expect to walk five miles? Wait, lem'mesee," he added, dismounting from his horse and coming towards her, and speaking with good-natured gruffness. "You young gals ain't worth much nohow; you was sorter made to be put in a glass case to be looked at."

"If the glass case happened to be on this vehicle

it would have been smashed long ago," said Ellen, too low to elicit an answer from her companion, who went on examining her situation.

"Well now, seems to me that orter be easy as a rocking-chair jest down in that hollow, with this log on this side en' that plank at the back. These nails is a little inconvenient to the back, but I call fix that comfortable for you."

"Oh, thank you," said Ellen earnestly, looking with horror upon a return to the seat of torture; "I do not think I can try it again. Let me walk, and you can bring my trunk for me."

But upon being lifted down she found herself so bruised and lamed from the ride that she could only totter to the side of the road, where she sank down, and all of her courage deserting her, she burst into tears.

"Tut, tut, tut," said the old man, really distressed to see her troubled; "well now, that's too bad! Stop, wait; could you ride behind me on the horse? That would be easier-like."

Interpreting her hesitation rightly as a parley with herself as to the propriety of the move, he continued:

"Law! you wouldn't mind an old man like me, with has grandchildren old us you is; jest you try it. Old Dobbin he's as gentle as a sucking-pig and easy as a cradle."

Had there been any other resource, the young lady would have declined this offer; but there was no option. She could not walk, nor ride as she had been doing, so with the best grace she might she saw the old man fix his cloth coat on the horse for her to sit on, and then allowed herself to be drawn up after him, overcoming with an effort the fears of being kicked by the horse or run over by the wagon.

"Now don't mind me, jest you hold on tight; ef you don't you'll slip down in the road and git hurt," said her escort.

She did mind him, however, and it was only as she found the prediction of her slipping off into the road about to be verified that she clung to him as tightly as he could have wished. The old man chuckled merrily as he felt her slight arms tightening about him, but the only remark he made was:

"Gals is undoubtedly slippery critters, en' it takes a monsus tight hold to keep 'em in place. Why, Miss, when I was courtin' my Betsy Ann—that's my wife, Ma'am, who's got twenty-two grandchildren now—she give me the slip three individual times, owin' to Mike Simmons bein arter her too! en' it wasnt till I told her I was goin' to Texas that she cumroun', en' Mike wasn't nowhar."

Ellen strove to enjoy the joke to the same degree with the narrator, but the anxieties and hardships of the day were beginning to tell upon her spirits; and if the old man had possessed eyes in the back of his head, he would have seen her weeping silently behind the shield afforded by his back.

"So you say them Yankees vanquished you from home?" continued he after a silence of a few minutes.

"They is real rascals, that's a fact! What had you done?"

Ellen narrated, in as few words as she could, the substance of her adventures.

The interest of the story, on which he was forced to bestow his undivided attention in order to hear it, the rumbling of the wagon, and the fact that the broad back of the man intercepted the vision of Ellen Randolph, conspired to prevent either one of the parties from being conscious of an approaching horse, or from seeing that his rider, a young Confederate, was even now displaying no inconsiderable amount of interest in the tones of Ellen's voice, whose clear notes, raised to overcome her companion's infirmity, fell upon his ear when he was still some distance off.

It was curious to note the change which passed over his bronzed face as the first sound caught his attention; it spoke of recognition, astonishment, anxiety, and agitation. He first moderated the pace of his steed and then stoppod it entirely, listening intently. As the voice came nearer and nearer he caught the words:

"And they sent me from my home on half an hour's notice, under a guard of twenty-eight men."

"Miss Randof, eempossible!" said the horseman as the continued progress of the wagon brought it alongside of him, and the confirmation of his first conviction reached him in the familiar features of Ellen Randolph appearing from behind the person of her escort.

At the same moment her glance fell upon the face of Mr. Hautman. All unprepared as she was for his appearance, it is a mercy that she did not throw herself from the horse, which would have brought her directly under the wheels of the wagon. As it was, the old man found himself suddenly released from the clasp in which she had held him, and had only time to stop his horses by a jerk of the reins before the catastrophe occurred, and the young lady stood crying and exclaiming in the road:

"Oh, Mr. Hautman! Mr. Hautman! I am so glad!"

"What is de matter, my dear young lady?" said the gentlemen, dismounting and seizing her hand.

It was some time before the necessary explanations could be given, as Ellen was far too much excited, agitated, and embarrassed to attempt a very lucid account of herself; but sufficient was gathered from her incoherent expressions to give him a clue to the situation.

"Wait for me a minit," said the impulsive German, darting up the road a short distance and returning immediately. "I haf take a, leetel curse of de Yankees now, em' I feels better; but the Dievel will git Meelroy for dis, be sadeesfied on dat."

Ellen's laugh checked her tears at his comical earnestness of manner.

"I think, if I might choose. I would rather he would get Purdy;" said she. "I don't think Milroy was as active a mover in my expedition as he was."

"Well, he vill git bofe den," said Mr. Hautman, glad to see that she was recovering some of her old spirit.

But the journey to Mount Jackson must be continued. In vain Mr. Hautman contended for the privilege of substituting himself as her escort and the half of his horse as her mode of conveyance; for Ellen with strange obstinancy positively declined his offer, and declared her preference for her former arrangement. So the young gentleman was obliged to content himself with the second post of honor, by her side, from which position he managed to elicit the information he desired about herself and their mutual friends in Winchester, giving her in return a graphic account of his own adventures, particularly dwelling upon his visit to Rose Hill, where he had so successfully sustained the character of piano-tuner.

The rest of the ride to Mount Jackson proved much shorter than Ellen had any idea it would do. It is rather a pretty little village, with a background of mountains with the smiling fields and pretty, country-houses clotting the landscape between. At the entrance of the town were the large brown board hospital buildings erected by General Jackson, forming the first traces which Ellen had seen of the presence of the Southern army, and even that was a footprint of the past. The hotel was either more inviting in appearance, or Ellen was disposed to take a more cheerful view of everything now that she no longer felt herself alone. The kind-hearted old man who had lent her such material aid, took leave of his young charge with an empressment of manner which led Ellen to fear that he might attempt to act out his character of grandfather. He positively refused all remuneration for his services; and Ellen promised if she ever came down the valley again that she would hunt him out in his home among the hills, and make the acquaintance of "Betsy Ann."

Night had almost drawn her curtain as Ellen threw herself into an easy-chair in the little parlor, to wait until Mr. Hautman made some arrangements for a room for her. Still dreadfully wearied and bruised from her long journey, and almost sick from fasting, the sight of a familiar friendly face had turned the whole current of her feelings. A cheerful talk and a hearty laugh are at last the best tonic Nature affords, and this the bright, joyous temper of Mr. Hautman always gave her.

"Vill you go to your room now, or vait till supper?" said that gentleman, making his appearance after a few moments' absence.

"Oh, to my room by all means," said Ellen, glancing at her disordered attire; "though I shall be ready for my supper, and glad to get it, in a few minutes."

It was at this same supper that Ellen received her first lessons in Southern cookery. They were introduced into a long, low room with a table spread through its entire length, and around it were seated a motley crowd, mostly soldiers, though there was a light sprinkling of peaceable citizens and women. Ellen could not avoid a consciousness as she entered the room that she was the observed of all observers, as every eye turned upon her curiously, and it was with flaming cheeks that she gained her seat.

"Tea or coffee?" asked the waiter.

"Coffee," answered Ellen, inwardly rejoicing at the prospect of the stimulating beverage which would be so particularly grateful after her fatiguing journey. A cupful of liquid of promising appearance further excited her anticipations of enjoyment, which, however, were completely blasted by the first mouthful.

"What is it?" she asked, turning to Mr. Hautman, who was watching her dismay with intense enjoyment.

"Deed not you say to de waiter you want coffee?" he asked in pretended surprise.

"Yes," said Ellen in it low tone; "but I never tasted such stuff as this."

"Fy, it is de var best rye-coffee," said he, laughing.

"Well," said the young lady, still in a tone which could not extend beyond his ear, "I am very sorry, but I can't drink it. Ask the waiter for a cup of tea."

"Bring some tea to de lady," said Mr. Hautman, stopping a waiter who was hurrying past with all the self-importance which attaches to his peculiar profession.

"Sassafras or t'other?" said the man.

"Sassafras or t'oher!" repeated Ellen, feeling as if she had somehow chanced upon a people speaking a new language to her. "What does he mean?"

"He means," said Mr. Hautman, as soon as he could command himself sufficiently, "will you have sassafras tea or de udder?"

"Yes, ma'am," said the waiter, "Sassafras is the regular article; t'other is two dollars extra a cup."

"Bring me genuine tea," said Ellen, feeling greatly embarrassed at the mere mention of *price* before a gentleman."

"Genwine! Genwine!" said the man, thoughtfully. "We is jist out of dat article, Ma'am; 'spect, a new supply to-morrow."

This was too much for Mr. Hautman, whose explosive laugh startled everybody in the room.

"Bring de yong lady some t'udder den," said he, as soon as he could speak; and Ellen enjoyed a very palatable cup of green tea in spite of the brown sugar sweetening to which she was obliged to submit.

Notwithstanding her fatigue it was a long time after Ellen had retired to rest before she could so command the bewildering maze of thought which beset her brain as to go to sleep; and in the midst of the chaos of trouble and anxiety, the pleasure of one meeting which had renewed a delightful past, one word which opened up a sweet future, had their places. I leave my reader to guess what they were.

Chapter XIII: The Seven Days' Battles

From *Reminiscences of Peace and War (1904)*

Mrs. Roger A. Pryor

THE intense heat of June 25th has been noted in many of the diaries and records of the day. I remember it because I had feared its unfavorable effect upon my husband, not yet discharged by his physicians, and now lying weak and listless upon his bed at the Spotswood Hotel in Richmond.

I was reading aloud to him the news in the morning papers, fanning him the while, when a peremptory knock at the door sent me to my feet. An ominous-looking note was handed in to "Brigadier-General Pryor." Upon reading it, my husband slipped to the side of the bed, and reached out for his cavalry boots. The note ran: "Dear General, put yourself at once at the head of your brigade. In thirty-six hours it will all be over. Longstreet." Before I realized the tremendous import of the order, he was gone.

McClellan was almost at the gates of the city. The famous "seven days' fight" was about to begin.

Several of the officers of our brigade were in the hotel, and I ran out to find their wives and learn more news from them. On the stair I met Colonel Scott, and as he passed me, he exclaimed, "No time until I come back, madam!" Turning, he paused, raised his hand, and said solemnly, "If I ever come back." The wife of Captain Poindexter came up at the moment. She was weeping, and wringing her hands. "Do you think," she said, "that we could drive out to camp and see them once more before they march?"

We hurried into the street, found a carriage, and, urging our driver to his utmost speed, were soon in sight of the camp.

All was hurry and confusion there. Ambulances were hitching up, troops forming in line, servants running hither and thither, horses standing to be saddled, light army wagons loading with various camp utensils.

Captain Whitner of the General's staff smiled at me, and said, as he conducted me to my husband's tent: "The General will be so glad to see you, Madam! He is lying down to rest a few minutes before we move."

He opened his arms to me as I went in, but there were no sad words. We spoke cheerily to each other, but, unable to control myself, I soon ran out to find John and see that he had provided brandy and cold tea, the latter a necessity lest good water should be unprocurable. Never have I seen such a number of flies! They blackened the land, corrupted the food, and tormented the nervous horses. When I returned, Mrs. Poindexter was standing outside the tent waiting for me. "I can see my husband only at the head of his company," she said. "Look! They are forming the line."

We stood aside as the brigade formed in marching order. The stern command, "Fall in! Fall in!" reached us from company after company stretching far down the road. My husband mounted his horse, and, drawing his sword, gave the order to advance.

We could not bear to remain a moment after they left. Finding our carriage, we were about to enter, when their driver pointed back with his whip. There, sure enough, rose the puffs of blue smoke from McClellan's guns — so near, so near!

We set our faces homeward, two stunned, tearless women, neither yet able to comfort the other. Presently the carriage stopped, and the driver, dismounting, came to the door.

"Lady," said he, "there's a man lying on the roadside. We just passed him. Maybe he's drunk, but he 'pears to me to look mighty sick."

Fanny Poindexter and I were out of the carriage in less than a minute, eagerly embracing an opportunity for action—the relief for tense feelings.

The man wore the uniform of a Confederate soldier. His eyes were closed. Was he asleep: we feared the worst when we perceived a thin thread of blood trickling slowly from a wound in his throat, and staining his shirt.

We knelt beside him, and Fanny gently pressed her handkerchief upon the wound, whereupon he opened his eyes, but was unable to speak. "What in the world are we to do?" said my friend. "We can't possibly leave him here!"

"I can tote him to the carriage," said the kindhearted driver. "He ain' no heavy-weight, an' we can car' 'im to dat hospital jus' at de aidge of town. Come now, sir! Don't you be feared. I'll tote you like a baby."

We were terrified lest he should die before we reached the hospital. To avoid jolting, we crawled at a snail's pace, and great was our relief when we drew up at the open door of the hospital and summoned a surgeon. He ordered out a stretcher and took our patient in, and we waited in a little reception room until we could learn the verdict after an examination of his injuries.

"It is well for him, poor fellow," said the surgeon upon returning to report to us, "that you found him when you did. His wound is not serious, but he was slowly bleeding to death! Which of you pressed that handkerchief to it?" I had to acknowledge that my friend had rendered this service. She was one of those nervous, teary little women who could rise to an occasion.

"He had probably been sent to the rear after he was wounded, and had tried to find General Pryor's camp," said the doctor. "He missed his way, and went farther than necessary. It has all turned out right. He is able now to write his name—'Ernstorff'—so you see he is doing well. When you pass this way, you must call and see him."

We never went that way again. Two years afterward I was accosted at a railway station by a handsome young officer who said he "had never forgotten, never would forget" me. He was Lieutenant Ernstorff!

All the afternoon the dreadful guns shook the earth and thrilled our souls with horror. I shut myself in my darkened room. At twilight I had a note from Governor Letcher, telling me a fierce battle was raging, and inviting me to come to the Governor's mansion. From the roof one might see the flash of musket and artillery.

No! I did not wish to see the infernal fires. I preferred to watch and wait alone in my room.

The city was strangely quiet. Everybody had gone out the hills to witness the aurora of death to which we were later to become so accustomed. As it grew dark a servant entered to light my candle, but I forbade her. Did I not mean to go to supper? I would have coffee brought to me. God only knew what news I might hear before morning. I must keep up my strength.

The night was hot and close. I sat at an open window, watching for couriers on the street. The firing ceased about nine o'clock. Surely now somebody would remember us and come to us.

As I leaned on the window-sill with my head on my arms, I saw two young men walking slowly down the deserted street. They paused at a closed door opposite me and sat down upon the low step. Presently they chanted a mournful strain in a minor key—like one of the occasional interludes of Chopin which reveal so much of dignity in sorrow. I was powerfully affected—as I always am by such music—and found myself weeping, not for my own changed life, not for my own sorrows, but for the dear city; the dear, doomed city, so loved, so loved!

A full moon was rising behind the trees in the Capitol Square. Soon the city would be flooded with light, and then!—would the invading host come in to desecrate and destroy: how dear the city had been to me always! I could remember when I was a very little child one just such night as this. The splendor, the immensity of the city had so oppressed me, coming, as I had come, from the quiet country, that I could not sleep. Hot and fevered and afraid, I had risen from my little bed beside my sleeping mother, and had stolen to the window to look out. Like to-night an awful stillness in the city. Just below me a watchman had called out, "all's well!" Presently the cry was repeated at a distance—"All's well!" Fainter and fainter grew the echo until it became a whisper, far away in the distant streets. The watchmen were telling me, I thought, telling all the helpless little babies and children, all the sick people and old people, that God was taking care of them; that "All's well, All's well."

Ah! Forever gone was the watchman, forever silent the cry. Never, never again could all be well with us in old Virginia. Never could we stifle the memories of this bitter hour. The watchman on the nation's tower might, some day, mark the triumphant return of this invading host, and declare, "All's well,"—our hearts would never hear. Too much blood, too much death, too much anguish! Our tears would never be able to wash away the memory of it all.

And so the night wore on and I waited and watched. Before dawn a hurried footstep brought a message from the battle-field to my door.

"The General, Madam, is safe and well. Colonel Scott has been killed. The General has placed a guard around his body, and he will be sent here early to-morrow. The General bids me say he will not return. The fight will be renewed, and will continue until the enemy is driven away."

My resolution was taken. My children were safe with their grandmother. I would write. I would ask that every particle of my household linen, except a change, should be rolled into bandages, all my fine linen be sent to me for compresses, and all forwarded as soon as possible.

I would enter the new hospital which had been improvised in Kent & Paine's warehouse, and would remain there as a nurse as long as the armies were fighting around Richmond.

But the courier was passing on his rounds with news for others. Presently Fanny Poindexter, in tears, knocked at my door.

"She is bearing it like a brave, Christian woman."

"She! Who?: Tell me quick."

"Mrs. Scott. I had tell her. She simply said, 'I shall see him once more.' The General wrote to her from the battle-field and told her how nobly her husband died, — leading his men in the thick of the fight, — and how he had helped to save the city."

Alas, that the city should have needed saving! What had Mrs. Scott and her children done?: Why should they suffer?: Who was to blame for it all?

Kent & Paine's warehouse was a large, airy building, which had, I understood, been offered by the proprietors for a hospital immediately after the battle of Seven Pines. McClellan's advance upon Richmond had heavily taxed the capacity of the hospitals already established.

When I reached the warehouse, early on the morning after the fight at Mechanicsville, I found cots on the lower floor already occupied, and other cots in process of preparation. An aisle between the rows of narrow beds stretched to the rear of the building. Broad stairs led to a story above, where other cots were being laid.

The volunteer matron was a beautiful Baltimore woman, Mrs. Wilson. When I was presented to her as a candidate for admission, her serene eyes rested doubtfully upon me for a moment. She hesitated. Finally she said: "The work is very exacting. There are so few of us that our nurses must do anything and everything — make beds, wait upon anybody, and often a half a dozen at a time."

"I will engage to do all that," I declared, and she permitted me to go to a desk at the farther end of the room and enter my name.

As I passed by the rows of occupied cots, I saw a nurse kneeling beside one of them, holding a pan for a surgeon. The red stump of an amputated arm was held over it. The next thing I knew I was myself lying on a cot, and a spray of cold water was falling over my face. I had fainted. Opening my eyes, I found the matron standing beside me.

"You see it is as I thought. You are unfit for this work. One of the nurses will conduct you home."

The nurse's assistance was declined, however. I had given trouble enough for one day, and had only interrupted those who were really worth something.

A night's vigil had been poor preparation for hospital work. I resolved I would conquer my culpable weakness. It was all very well, — these heroics in which I indulged, these paroxysms of patriotism, this adoration of the defenders of my fireside. The defender in the field had naught to hope from me in case he should be wounded in my defence.

I took myself well in hand. Why had I fainted? I thought it was because of the sickening, dead odor in the hospital, mingled with that of acids and disinfectants. Of course this will always be there — and worse, as wounded men filled the rooms. I provided myself with sal volatile and spirits of camphor, — we wore pockets in our gowns in those days, — and thus armed I presented myself again to Mrs. Wilson.

She was as kind as she was refined and intelligent. "I will give you a place near the door," she said, "and you must run out into the air at the first hint of faintness. You will get over it, see if you don't."

Ambulances began to come in and unload at the door. I soon had occupation enough, and a few drops of camphor on my handkerchief tided me over the worst. The wounded men crowded in and sat patiently waiting their turn. One fine little fellow of fifteen unrolled a handkerchief from his wrist to show me his wound. "There's a bullet in there," he said proudly. "I'm going to have it cut out, and then go right back to the fight. Isn't it lucky it's my left hand?"

As the day wore on I became more and more absorbed in my work. I had, too, the stimulus of a reproof from Miss Deborah Couch, a brisk, efficient middle-aged lady, who asked no quarter and gave none. She was standing beside me a moment, with a bright tin pan filled with pure water, into which I foolishly dipped a finger to see if it were warm; to learn if I would be expected to provide warm mater when I should be called upon to assist the surgeon.

"This water, Madam, was prepared for a raw wound," said Miss Deborah, sternly. "I must now make the surgeon wait until I get more."

Miss Deborah, in advance of her time, was a germ theorist. My touch evidently was contaminating.

As she charged down the aisle with a pan of water in her hand, everybody made way. She had none of my "fine-lady faintness," as she termed it, and I could see she despised me for it. She had volunteered, as all the nurses had, and she meant business. She had no patience with nonsense, and truly she was worth more than all the rest of us.

"Where can I get a little ice?" I one day ventured of Miss Deborah.

"Find it," she rejoined, as she rapidly passed on, but find it I never did. Ice was an unknown luxury until brought to us later from private houses.

But I found myself thoroughly reinstated— with surgeons, matrons, and Miss Deborah—when I appeared a few days later, accompanied by a man bearing a basket of clean, well-rolled bandage, with promise of more to come. The Petersburg women had gone to work with a will upon my table-cloths, sheets, and dimity counterpanes — and even the chintz furniture covers. My springlike green and white chintz bandages appeared on many a manly arm and leg. My fine linen underwear and napkins were cut, but the sewing circle at the Spotswood, according to the surgeon's directions, into lengths two inches wide, then folded two inches, doubling back and forth in a smaller fold each time, until they formed pointed wedges for compresses.

Such was the sudden and overwhelming demand for such things, that but for my own and similar donations of household linen, the wounded men would have suffered. The war had come upon us suddenly. Many of our ports were already closed, and we had no stores laid up for such an emergency.

The bloody battle of Gaines's Mill soon followed — then Frazier's Farm, within the week and at once the hospital was filled to overflowing. Every night a courier brought me tidings of my husband. When I saw him at the door my heart would die within me! One morning John came in for certain supplies. After being reassured as to his master's safety, I asked, "Did he have a comfortable night, John?"

"He sholy did! Marse Roger cert'nly was comfortable las' night. He slep' on de field 'twist two daid horses!"

The women who worked in Kent & Paine's hospital never seemed to weary. After a while the wise matron assigned us hours, and we went on duty with the regularity of trained nurses. My hours were from seven to seven during the day, with the promise of night service should I be needed. Efficient, kindly colored women assisted us. Their motherly manner soothed the prostrate soldier, whom they always addressed as "son."

Many fine young fellows lost their lives for want of prompt attention. They never murmured.

They would give way to those who seemed to be more seriously wounded than themselves, and the latter would recover, while from the slighter wound gangrene would supervene from delay. Very few men ever walked away from that hospital. They died, or friends found quarters for them in the homes in Richmond. None complained! Unless a poor man grew delirious, he never groaned. There was an atmosphere of gentle kindness, a suppression of emotion for the sake of others.

Every morning the Richmond ladies brought for our patients such luxuries as could be procured in that scarce time. The city was in peril, and distant farmers feared to bring in their fruits and vegetables. One day a patient-looking middle-aged man said to me, "What would I not give for a bowl of chicken broth like that my mother used to give me when I was a sick boy!" I perceived one of the angelic matrons of Richmond at a distance, stooping over the cots, and found my way to her and said: "Dear Mrs. Maben, have you a chicken? And could you send some broth to No. 39?" She promised, and I returned with her promise to the poor wounded fellow. He shook his head. "To-morrow will be too late," he said.

I had forgotten the circumstance next day, but at noon I happened to look toward cot No. 39, and there was Mrs. Maben herself. She had brought the chicken broth in a pretty china bowl, with napkin and silver spoon, and was feeding my doubting Thomas, to his great satisfaction.

It was at this hospital, I have reason to believe, that the little story originated, which was deemed good enough to be claimed by other hospitals, of the young girl who approached a sick man with a pan of water in her hand and a towel over her arm.

"Mayn't I wash your face?" said the girl, timidly. "Well, lady, you may if you want to," said the man, wearily. "It has been washed fourteen times this morning! It can stand another time, I reckon."

I discovered that I had not succeeded, despite many efforts, in winning Miss Deborah. I learned that she was affronted because I had not shared my offerings of jelly and fruit with her, for her special patients. Whenever I ventured to ask a loan from her, of a pan or a glass for water or the little things of which we never had enough, she would reply, "I must keep them for the nurses who understand reciprocity. Reciprocity is a rule some persons never seem to comprehend." When this was hammered into my slow perception, I rose to the occasion. I turned over the entire contents of a basket the landlord of the Spotswood had given me to Miss Deborah, and she made my path straight before me ever afterward.

At the end of a week the matron had promoted me! Instead of carving the fat bacon, to be dispensed with corn bread, for the hospital dinner, or standing between two rough men to keep away the flies, or fetching water, or spreading sheets on cots, I was assigned to regular duty with one patient.

The first of these proved to be young Colonel Coppens, of my husband's brigade. I could comfort him very little, for he was wounded past recovery. I spoke little French, and could only try to keep him, as far as possible, from annoyance. To my great relief, a place was found for him in a private family. There he soon died — the gallant fellow I had admired on his horse a few months before.

Then I was placed beside the cot of Mr. (or Captain) Boyd of Mecklenburg, and was admonished by the matron not to leave him alone. He was the most patient sufferer in the old, gentle, courteous, always considerate, never complaining. I observed he often closed his eyes and sighed. "Are you in pain, Captain?" "No, no," he would say gently. One day, when I returned from my "rest," I found the matron sitting beside him. Tears were running down her cheeks. She motioned me take her place, and then added, "No, no, I will not leave him."

The Captain's eyes were closed, and he sighed wearily at intervals. Presently he whispered slowly:—

"There everlasting spring abides," then sighed, and seemed to sleep for a moment.

The matron felt his pulse and raised a warning hand. The sick man's whisper went on:—

"Bright fields beyond the swelling flood
Stand-dressed-in living green."

The surgeon stood at the foot of the cot and shook his head. The nurses gathered around with tearful eyes. Presently in clear tones:—

"not Jordan's stream-nor death's cold flood
Shall fright us-from-the shore,"

And in a moment more the Christian soldier had crossed the river and lain down to rest under the trees.

Each of the battles of those seven days brought a harvest of wounded to our hospital. I used to veil myself closely as I walked to and from my hotel, that I might shut out the dreadful sights in the street,—the squads of prisoners and, worst of all, the open wagons in which the dead were piled. Once I did see one of these dreadful wagons! In it a stiff arm was raised, and shook as it was driven down the street, as though the dead owner appealed to heaven for vengeance; a horrible sight never to be forgotten.

After one of the bloody battles—I know not if it was Gaine's Mill or Frazier's Farm or Malvern Hill—a splendid young officer, Colonel Brokenborough, was taken to our hospital, shot almost to pieces. He was borne up the stairs and placed in a cot—his broken limbs in supports swinging from the ceiling. The wife of General Mahone and I were permitted to assist in nursing him. A young soldier from the camp was detailed to help us, and a clergyman was in constant attendance, coming at night that we might rest. Our patient held a court in his corner of the hospital. Such a dear, gallant, cheery fellow, handsome, and with a grand air even as he lay prostrate! Nobody ever heard him complain. He would welcome us in the morning with the brightest smile. His aide said, "He watches the head of the stairs and calls up that look for your benefit." "Oh," he said one day, "you can't guess what's going to happen! Some ladies have been here and left all these roses, and cologne, and such; and somebody has sent champagne! We are going to have a party!"

Ah, but we knew he was very ill! We were bidden to watch him every minute and not be deceived by his own spirits. Mrs. Mahone spent her life hunting for ice. My constant care was to keep his canteen—to which he clung with affection—filled with fresh water from a spring not far away, and I learned to give it to him so well that I allowed no one to lift his head for his drink during my hours.

One day, when we were alone, I was fanning him, and thought he was asleep. He said gravely, "Mrs. Pryor, beyond that curtain they hung up yesterday poor young Mitchell is lying! They think I don't know! But I heard when they brought him in,—as I lie here, I listen to his breathing. I haven't heard it now for some time. Would you mind seeing if he is all right?"

I passed behind the curtain. The young soldier was dead. His wide-open eyes seemed to meet mine in mute appeal. I had never seen or touched a dead man, but I laid my hands upon his eyelids and closed them. I was standing thus when his nurse, a young volunteer like myself, came to me.

"I couldn't do that," she said; "I went for the doctor. I'm so glad you could do it."

When I returned Colonel Brokenborough asked no questions and I knew that his keen senses had already instructed him.

To be cheerful and uncomplaining was the unwritten law of our hospital. No bad news was ever mentioned, no foreboding or anxiety. Mrs. Mahone was one day standing beside Colonel Brokenborough when a messenger from the front suddenly announced that General Mahone had received a flesh-wound. Commanding herself instantly, she exclaimed merrily: "Flesh-wound! Now you all know that is just impossible." The General had no flesh! He was as thin and attenuated as he was brave.

As Colonel Brokenborough grew weaker I felt self-reproach that no one had offered to write letters for him. His friend the clergyman had said to me: "That poor boy is engaged to a lovely young girl. I wonder what is best? Would it grieve him to speak of her? You ladies have so much tact; you might bear it in mind. An opportunity might offer for you to discover how he feels about it." The next time I was alone with him I ventured: "Now, Colonel, one mustn't forget absent friends, you know, even if fair ladies do bring perfumes and roses and what not. I have some ink and paper here. Shall I write a letter for you? Tell me what to say."

He turned his head and with a half-amused smile of perfect intelligence looked at me for a long time. Then an upward look of infinite tenderness; but the message was never sent—never needed from a true heart like his.

One night I was awakened from my first sleep by a knock at my door, and a summons to "come to Colonel Brokenborough." When I reached his bedside I found the surgeon, their clergyman, and the Colonel's aide. The patient was unconscious; the end was near. We sat in silence. Once, when he stirred, I slipped my hand under his head, and put his canteen once more to his lips. After a long time his breathing simply ceased, with no evidence of pain. We waited awhile, and then the young soldier who had been detailed to nurse him rose, crossed the room, and, stooping over, kissed me on my forehead, and went out to his duty in the ranks.

Two weeks later I was in my room, resting after a hard day, when a haggard officer, covered with mud and dust, entered. It was my husband.

"My men are all dead," he said, with anguish, and falling across the bed, he gave vent to the passionate grief of his heart.

Thousands of confederate soldiers were killed, thousands wounded.

Richmond was saved!

General McClellan and General Lee both realized that their men needed rest. My husband was allowed a few days' respite from duty. Almost without pause he had fought the battles of Williamsburg, Seven Pines, Mechanicsville, Gaine's Mill, and Frazier's Farm. He had won his promotion early, but he had lost the loved commander who appreciated him, had seen old schoolmates and friends fall by his side, — the dear fellow, George Loyal Gordon, who had been his best man at our wedding, — old college comrades, valued old neighbors.

Opposed to him in battle, then and after, were men who in after years avowed themselves his warm friends, — General Hancock, General Slocum, General Butterfield, General Sickles, General Fitz-John Porter, General McClellan, and General Grant. They had fought loyally under opposing banners, and from time to time, as the war went on, one and another had been defeated; but overall, and through all, their allegiance had been given to a banner that has never surrendered, — the standard of the universal brotherhood of all true men.

August 1864

From *The Diary of a Southern Refugee, During the War, By a Lady of Virginia* (1867)

Judith W. McGuire

AUGUST 11th. —Sheridan's and Early's troops are fighting in the Valley. We suffered a disaster near Martinsburg, and our troops fell back to Strasburg; had a fight on the old battle-ground at Kernstown, and we drove the enemy through Winchester to Martinsburg, which our troops took possession of. Poor Winchester, how checkered its history throughout the war! Abounding with patriotism as it is, what a blessing it must be to have a breath of free air, even though it be for a short time! Their welcome of our soldiers is always so joyous, so bounding, so generous! How they must enjoy the blessed privilege of speaking their own sentiments without having their servants listening and acting as spies in their houses, and of being able to hear from or write to their friends! Oh! I would that there was a prospect of their being disenthralled forever.

12th. —I am sorry to record a defeat near Moorfield, in Hardy County. These disasters are very distressing to us all, except to the croakers, who find in them so much food for their gloom, that I am afraid they are rather pleased than otherwise. They always, on such occasions, elongate their mournful countenances, prophesy evil, and chew the cud of discontent with a better show of reason than they can generally produce.

The signal failure of Grant's mine to blow up our army, and its recoil upon his own devoted troops, amply repay us for our failure in Hardy. God's hand was in it, and to Him be the praise.

One of my friends in the office is a victim of Millroy's reign in Winchester. She wrote to a friend of hers at the North, expressing her feelings rather imprudently. The letter was intercepted, and she was immediately arrested, and brought in an ambulance through the enemy's lines to our picket-post, where she was deposited by the roadside. She says that she was terribly distressed at leaving her mother and sisters, but when she got into Confederate lines the air seemed wonderfully fresh, pure and free, and she soon found friends. She came to Richmond and entered our office. About the same time a mother and daughters who lived perhaps in the handsomest house in the town, were arrested, for some alleged imprudence of one of the daughters. An ambulance was driven to the door, and the mother was taken from her sick-bed and put into it, together with the daughters. Time was not allowed them to prepare a lunch for the journey. Before Mrs. was taken from her house, Mrs. Millroy had entered it, the General having taken it for his head-quarters; and before the ambulance had been driven off, one of their own officers was heard to say to Mrs. M., seeing her so entirely at home in the house, "For goodness' sake, madam, wait until the poor woman gets off." Is it wonderful, then, that the Winchester ladies welcome our troops with gladness? That they rush out and join the band, singing "The bonnie blue flag" and "Dixie," as the troops enter the streets, until their enthusiasm and melody melt all hearts? Was it strange that even the great and glorious, though grave and thoughtful, Stonewall Jackson should, when pursuing Banks through its streets, have been excited until he waved his cap with tears of enthusiasm, as they broke forth in harmonious songs of welcome? Or that the ladies, not being satisfied by saluting them with their voices, waving their handkerchiefs, and shouting for joy, should follow them with more substantial offerings, filling their haversacks with all that their depleted pantries could afford? Or is it wonderful that our soldiers should love Winchester so dearly and fight for it so valiantly? No, it is beautiful to contemplate the long-suffering, the firmness under oppression, the patience, the generosity, the patriotism of Winchester. Other towns, I dare say, have borne their tyranny as well, and when their history is known they will call forth our admiration as much; but we *know* of no such instance. The "Valley" throughout shows the same devotion to our cause, and the sufferings of the country people are even greater than those in town.

Some amusing incidents sometimes occur, showing the eagerness of the ladies to serve our troops after a long separation. A lady living near Berryville, but a little remote from the main road, says, that when our troops are passing through the country, she sometimes feels sick with anxiety to do something for them. She, one morning, stood in her porch, and could see them turn in crowds to neighbouring houses—which happened to be on the road, but no one turned out of the way far enough to come to her house. At last one man came along, and finding that he was passing her gate, she ran out with the greatest alacrity to invite him to come in to get his breakfast. He turned to her with an amused expression and replied: "I am much obliged to you, madam; I wish I could breakfast with you, but as I have already eaten our breakfasts to please the ladies, I must beg you to excuse me."

14th. —Norfolk, poor Norfolk! nothing can exceed its long-suffering, its night of gloom and darkness. Unlike Winchester, it has no bright spots—no oasis in its blank desert of wretchedness. Like Alexandria, it has no relief, but must submit, and drag on its chain of servility, till the final cry of victory bursts its bonds, and makes it Free. I have no time to write of all I hear and know of the indignities offered to our countrymen and countrywomen in Alexandria, Norfolk, Portsmouth, and other places which remain incarcerated in the sloughs of Federal tyranny. God help them, and give us strength speedily to break the chain that binds them.

August 15th. — An account from my relatives, of the raid of the 19th of June into the village of Tappahannock, has lately reached me. The village had been frequently visited and pillaged before, and both sides of the beautiful Rappahannock, above and below, had been sadly devastated; but the last visit seems to carry with it more of the spirit of revenge than any before. My aunt writes:

"About daybreak on that peaceful Sabbath morn six gunboats were seen returning down the river. A rumour that Hampton was after them, had driven them from their work of devastation in the country above us to their boats for safety. By six o'clock six hundred negroes and four hundred cavalry and marines were let loose upon the defenceless town. The first visit I received was from six cavalrymen; the pantry-door was unceremoniously broken open, and a search made for wine and plate; but all such things had been removed to a place of safety, and when I called loudly for an officer to be sent for, the ruffians quietly went to their horses and departed. Next came a surgeon from Point Lookout, to search the house, and deliver the key to Dr. R's store, which he had sent for as soon as he landed—making a great virtue of his not breaking open the door, and of his honesty in only taking a few pills. This dignitary walked through the rooms, talking and murdering the 'king's English' most ludicrously. However, he behaved quite well through the day, and was, under Heaven, the means of protecting us from aggressions by his frequent visits. In a short time every unoccupied house in the village was forcibly entered, and every thing taken from them or destroyed. Dr. R's house was completely sacked. L. had made all necessary preparations for returning home, but all was swept by the Vandals. Dr. R's surgical instruments, books, medicines, his own and his sister's clothes, as well as those of their dead parents, were taken, the officers sharing the plunder with the soldiers. The furniture, such as was not broken up, was carried off in dray-loads to the boats, and these two young people were as destitute of domestic comforts as though a consuming fire had passed over their pleasant residence. My lot was filled with the creatures going in and out at pleasure, unless the cry, 'The Johnnies are coming,' sent them running like scared beasts to their rendezvous, and gave us a few moments of quiet. The poor negroes belonging to the town seemed to lose all power over themselves, and to be bereft of reason. Some seemed completely brutalized by the suggestions that were constantly whispered in their ears; others so frightened by the threats made, that reason deserted them; others so stupefied that they lost all power to direct themselves, and gave up to the control of others. It is impossible to describe the madness that possessed them. For myself, I had but one care left—to keep them from polluting my house any farther by keeping them out; and this I was enabled to do after shutting and locking the door in the face of one of them. The most painful event of the day was when a little coloured girl, a great pet with us, was dragged from the house. The aunt of the child was determined to take her with her, but she resisted all her aunt's efforts, and came to the house for protection. An officer came for her, and after talking with her, and telling her that he would not 'trouble her, but she was not old enough to know what was good for her,' he went off. About night a white man and the most fiendish-looking negro I ever saw came for her in the name of the aunt, and vowed they would have her at all risks.

"The officers had all gone to the boats, and

it was in vain to resist them, and with feelings of anguish we saw the poor child dragged from us. I cannot think of this event without pain. But night now set in, and our apprehensions increased as the light disappeared; we knew not what was before us, or what we should be called on to encounter during the hours of darkness. We only knew that we were surrounded by lawless banditti, from whom we had no reason to expect mercy, much less kindness; but above all, there was an eye that never slumbered, and an arm mighty to defend those who trusted to it, so we made the house as secure as we could, and kept ready a parcel of *sharp case-knives* (don't laugh at our weapons) for our defence, if needed, and went up-stairs, determined to keep close vigils all night. Our two faithful servants, Jacob and Anthony, kept watch in the kitchen. Among the many faithless, those two stood as examples of the comfort that good servants can give in time of distress. About nine o'clock we heard the sound of horses' feet, and Jacob's voice under the window. Upon demanding to know what was the matter, I was answered by the voice of a gun-boat captain, in broken German, that they were going to fire over my house at the 'Rebs' on the hill, and that we had better leave the house, and seek protection in the streets. I quietly told our counsellor that I preferred remaining in my own house, and should go to the basement, where we should be safe. So we hastily snatched up blankets and comforts, and repaired to the basement, where pallets were spread, and G's little baby laid down to sleep, sweetly unconscious of our fears and troubles. We sent to apprise the Misses G. of the danger, and urge them to come to us. They came, accompanied by an ensign, who had warded off danger from them several times during the day. He was a grave, middle-aged man, and was very kind. At the request of the ladies, he came into the room with us and remained until twelve o'clock. He was then obliged to return to the gun-boat, but gave us an efficient guard until daybreak. He pronounced Captain Schultz's communication false, as they had no idea of firing. We knew at once that the object had been to rob the house, as all unoccupied houses were robbed with impunity. This gentleman's name was Nelson. I can never forget his kindness. During the night our relative, Mrs. B., came to us in great agitation; she had attempted to stay at home, though entirely alone, to protect her property. She had been driven from her house at midnight, and chased across several lots to the adjoining one, where she had fallen from exhaustion. Jacob, hearing cries for help, went to her, and brought her to us. Our party now consisted of twelve females of all ages. As soon as the guard left us at daybreak, they came in streams to the hen-yard, and woe to the luckless chicken who thought itself safe from robbers! At one o'clock on Monday the fleet of now eight steamers took its departure. Two of the steamers were filled with the deluded negroes who were leaving their homes. We felt that the incubus which had pressed so heavily upon us for thirty hours had been removed, and we once more breathed freely, but the village was left desolate and destitute."

18th. — For several days our whole time has been occupied nursing the dear little grandchild, whose life was despaired of for two days. We are most thankful for his recovery.

The army is now on the north side of James River, and this evening, at this moment, we hear heavy cannonading, and musketry is distinctly heard from the hills around the city. Oh, Heavenly Father! Guide our generals and troops, and cause this sanguinary conflict to end by a desirable, an honourable peace!

20th. — A friend from the Valley has described a successful attack made by Mosby on a Federal wagon-train near Berryville. It was on its way to the army near Strasburg, and Mosby was on the other side of the Shenandoah. He crossed in the night with one cannon and about seventy-five men, and at daylight surprised the drivers and guard as they were beginning to hitch their mules, by a salute from the cannon and seventy-five pistols. There was a general stampede in an instant of all who were unhurt. As quick as thought, 600 mules were turned towards the river, and driven to the command in Loudoun. In the mean time, the wagons were set on fire, and most of them and their contents were consumed before the luckless drivers could return to their charge.

It is said that our new steamer, the "Tallahassee," has been within sixty miles of the city of New York, very much to the terror of the citizens. It also destroyed six large vessels. I bid it God-speed with all my heart; I want the North to feel the war to its core, and then it will end, and not before.

22nd. — Just been on a shopping expedition for my sister and niece, and spent $1,500 in about an hour. I gave $110 for ladies' morocco boots; $22 per yard for linen; $5 apiece for spools of cotton; $5 for a paper of pins, etc. It would be utterly absurd, except that it is melancholy, to see our currency depreciating so rapidly.

31st. — The last day of this exciting, troubled summer of 1864. How many young spirits have fled — how many bleeding, breaking hearts have been left upon earth, from the sanguinary work of this summer! Grant still remains near Petersburg; still by that means is he besieging Richmond. He has been baffled at all points, and yet his indomitable perseverance knows no bounds. Sherman still besieges Atlanta. God help us!

We are again troubled in mind and body about engaging rooms; we find we must give up these by the 1st of October, and have begun the usual refugee occupation of roomhunting.

Letters from our friends in the Valley, describing the horrors now going on there. A relative witnessed the burning of three very large residences on the 20th of August. General Custer was stationed with his brigade of Michigan Cavalry near Berryville. He had thrown out pickets on all the roads, some of which were fired on by Mosby's men. This so exasperated the Federals, that an order was at once issued that whenever a picket-post was fired on the nearest house should be burned. On the morning of the 20th this dreadful order was put into execution, and three large houses were burnt to the ground, together with barns, wheat-stacks, and outhouses. The house of Mr. was near a picket-post, and about midnight on the 19th a messenger arrived with a note announcing the sudden death of Mrs.'s sister, on a plantation not many miles distant. A lamp was lighted to read the note, and, unfortunately, a little while afterwards the picket-post was fired on and one man wounded. The lighting of the lamp was regarded as a signal to Colonel Mosby. During the same night the pickets near two other large houses were fired on. This being reported at head-quarters, the order was at once issued to burn all three houses. Two companies of the Fifth Michigan Cavalry, commanded by Captain Drake, executed the fearful order. They drew up in front of Mr.'s house and asked for him. "Are you Mr. *V*," demanded the Captain. "I have orders to burn your house." In vain Mr. remonstrated. He begged for one hour, that he might see General Custer and explain the circumstances of the night before; he also pleaded the illness of his son-in-law, then in the house. No reply was vouchsafed to the old gentleman, but with a look of hardened ferocity, he turned to the soldiers, with the order: "Men, to your work, and do it thoroughly!" In an instant the torch was applied to that home of domestic elegance and comfort. One soldier seized the sick son-in-law, who is a surgeon in our service, threatening to carry him to head-quarters, and was with difficulty prevented by the kind interposition of Dr. Sinclair, the surgeon of the regiment. They allowed the family to save as much furniture as they could but the servants were all gone, and there was no one near to help them. The soldiers at once went to Mr.'s secretary, containing $40,000 in bonds, destroyed it, and scattered the mutilated papers to the winds. Matches were applied to window and bed curtains; burning coals were sprinkled in the linen-closet, containing every variety of house and table linen. Mrs., the daughter, opened a drawer, and taking her jewelry, embracing an elegant diamond ring and other valuables, was escaping with them to the yard, when she was seized by two ruffians on the stair-steps, held by the arms by one, while the other forcibly took the jewels; they then, as she is a very small woman, lifted her over the banister and let her drop into the passage below; fortunately it was not very far and she was not at all injured. Nothing daunted, she rushed up-stairs, to rescue a box containing her bridal presents of silver, which was concealed in the wall above a closet. She climbed up to the highest shelf of the closet, seized the box, and, with unnatural strength, threw it through the window into the yard below. While still on the shelf, securing other things from their hiding-place, all unconscious of danger, a soldier set fire to some dresses hanging on the pegs below the shelf on which she stood. The first intimation she had of it was feeling the heat; she then leaped over the flames to the floor; her stockings were scorched, but she was not injured. She next saw a man with the sign of the Cross on his coat; she asked him if he was a chaplain? He replied that he was. She said, "Then in mercy come, and help me to save some of my mother's things." They went into her mother's chamber, and she hurriedly opened the bureau drawer, and began taking out the clothes, the chaplain assisting, but what was her horror to see him putting whatever he fancied into his pocket—among other things a paper of pins. She says she could not help saying, as she turned to him, "A minister of Christ stealing pins!!" In a moment the chaplain was gone, but the pins were returned to the bureau. Mrs. is the only daughter of Mr., and was the only lady on the spot. Her first care, when she found the house burning, was to secure her baby, which was sleeping in its cradle up-stairs. A guard was at the foot of the steps, and refused to let her pass; she told him that she was going to rescue her child from the flames. "Let the little rebel burn!" was the brutal reply. But his bayonet could not stop her; she ran by, and soon returned, bearing her child to a place of safety. When the house had become a heap of ruins, the mother returned from the bedside of her dead sister, whither she had gone at daylight that morning on horseback (for her harness had been destroyed by the enemy, making her carriage useless). She was, of course, overwhelmed with grief and with horror at the scene before her. As soon as she dismounted, a soldier leaped on the horse, and rode off with it. Their work of destruction in one place being now over, they left it for another scene of vengeance.

The same ceremony of Captain Drake's announcing his orders to the mistress of the mansion (the master was a prisoner) being over, the torch was applied. The men had dismounted; the work of pillage was going on merrily; the house was burning in every part, to insure total destruction. The hurried tramp of horses' feet could not be heard amidst the crackling of flames and falling of rafters, but the sudden shout and cry of "No quarter! no quarter!" from many voices, resounded in the ears of the unsuspecting marauders as a death-knell. A company of Mosby's men rushed up the hill and charged them furiously; they were aroused by the sound of danger, and fled hither and thither. Terrified and helpless, they were utterly unprepared for resistance. The cry of "No quarter! no quarter!" still continued. They hid behind the burning ruins; they crouched in the corners of fences; they begged for life; but their day of grace was past. The defenceless women, children, and old men of the neighbourhood had borne their tortures too long; something must be done, and all that this one company of braves could do, was done. Thirty were killed on the spot, and others, wounded and bleeding, sought refuge, and asked pity of those whom they were endeavouring to ruin. Two came to us, the most pitiable objects you ever beheld, and we did what we could for them; for, after all, the men are not to blame half so much as the officers. Whether these things have been ordered by Sheridan or Custer, we do not know. These two wounded men, and all who took refuge among Secessionists, were removed that night, contrary to our wishes, for we knew that their tortures in the ambulances would be unbearable; but they were unwilling to trust them, and unable to believe that persons who were suffering so severely from them could return good for evil.

"One man gruffly remarked: 'If we leave any of them with you all, Mosby will come and kill them over again.' We have since heard that those two men died that night. The pickets were then drawn in nearer to head quarters. All was quiet for the rest of the day, and as Colonel Mosby had but one company in that section of the country, it had of course retired. That night, two regiments (for they could not trust themselves in smaller numbers) were seen passing along the road; their course was marked by the torches which they carried. They rode to the third devoted house, and burned it to the ground. No one knows whose house will be the next object of revenge. Some fancied wrong may make us all homeless. We keep clothes, houselinen, and every thing compressible, tied up in bundles, so that they can be easily removed."

Such are some of the horrors that are being enacted in Virginia at this time. These instances, among many, many others, I note in my diary, that my children's children may know what we suffered during this unnatural war. Sheridan does not mean that Hunter or Butler shall bear the palm of cruelty—honours will at least be divided. I fear, from appearances, that he will exceed them, before his reign of terror is over. Ms. says she feels as if she were nightly encircled by fire—camp-fires, picket-fires, with here and there stacks of wheat burning, and a large fire now and then in the distance, denote the destruction of something—it may be a dwelling, or it may be a barn.

Chapter XXIII

From *My Day, Reminiscences of a Long Life* (1909)

Mrs. Roger A. Pryor

IN the colony escaped from the shells and huddled together around General Lee were two very humble poor women who often visited me. One of them was the proud owner of a cow, "Morning-Glory," which she contrived to feed from the refuse of the camp kitchens, receiving in return a small quantity of milk, to be sold at prices beyond belief. I never saw Morning-Glory, but I often heard her friendly echo to the lowing of my little Rose, morning and evening. Being interpreted, it might have been found to convey an expression of surprise that either was still alive, so slender was their allowance of food.

One day I espied, coming down the dusty road, the limp, sunbonneted figure of Morning-Glory's mistress. She sank upon the nearest chair, pushed back her calico bonnet, and revealed a face blurred with tears and hair dishevelled beyond the ordinary.

"Good morning, Mrs. Jones! Come to the fire! It's a cold morning."

"No'm, I ain't cole! It's—it's"—(sobbing)—"it's Mornin'-Glory!"

"Not sick? If she is, I'll—"

"No'm, Mornin'-Glory ain't never goin' to be sick no mo'."

"Oh, Mrs. Jones! *Not dead!*"

"Them pickets kep' me awake all las' night, an' I got up in the night an' went out to see how Mornin'-Glory was gettin' on, an' she—she—she look at me jus' the same! An' I slep' soun' till after sun-up, and when I got my pail an' went out to milk her—*thar was her horns an hufs!*"

The poor woman broke down completely in telling me the ghastly story. "Oh, how wicked! How was it possible to take her off and nobody hear?" I exclaimed in great wrath.

"I don't know, Mis' Pryor, nothin' but what I tells you. Talk to me 'bout Yankees! Soldiers is soldiers, an' when you say *that*, you jus' as well say devils is devils."

My other poor neighbor had long been a pensioner on my father. She was a forlorn widow with many children, hopeless and helpless. My father was in despair when she turned up "to git away from the shellin'." She found a small untenanted house near us and set up an establishment which was supported altogether by boarding an occasional soldier on sick leave, and taking his rations as her pay. Like Mrs. Jones, she was a frequent visitor to my fireside. One morning, after some unusual demonstrations of coy shyness, she blurted out: "I knows fo' I begin what you goin' to say! You goin' to tell me Ma'y Ann is a fool, an' I won't say you ain't in the rights of it."

"Well, what is Mary Ann's folly? I thought she had grown up to be a sensible girl."

"*Sensible! Ma'y Ann!* Them pretty gals is never sensible! No'm. Melissy Jane is the sensible one o' my chillun. I tole Ma'y Ann she didn't have nothin' fitten to be ma'ied in, an' she up an' say she know Mis' Pryor am' goin' to let one o' her pa's chu'ch people git ma'ied in rags."

"I certainly will not, Mrs. Davis! Mary Ann, I suppose, is to marry the soldier you've been taking care of. Tell her she may look to me for a wedding-dress. When is it to be?"

"Just as Dr. Pryor says — to-morrow if convenient."

I immediately overhauled the bundle of Washington finery and found a lavender Pina, or "pineapple" muslin, not yet prepared for sale. This was a delicate gown, trimmed with lavender silk, and with angel sleeves lined with white silk. This I sent to the prospective bride — considering her needs and station, a most unsuitable wedding garment, but all I had! I managed to make a contribution to the wedding supper, a large pumpkin I extorted from John, who had "found" it. Melissy Jane, homely enough to be brilliantly "sensible," appeared to take charge of the present, — the most slatternly, unlovely, and altogether unpromising of the poor white class I had ever seen; and my father, in view of the great good fortune coming to the forlorn family in the acquisition of an able-bodied, whole-hearted Confederate soldier, made no delay in performing the marriage ceremony. About a week afterward Mrs. Davis, limper than ever, more depressed than ever, reappeared.

"I hope nobody's sick?" I inquired.

"No'm, the chilluns is as peart as common. Ma'y Ann don't seem no ways encouraged. 'Pears like she's unreconciled."

"Why, what ails poor Mary Ann?"

"Yas'm — he's lef' her! Jus' took hisself off and never say nuthin'. We-all don't even know what company owns him."

"Mrs. Davis!" I exclaimed, in great indignation, "this is not to be tolerated. That man is to be found and made to do his duty. I can manage it!"

"I don't know as I keers to ketch 'im," sighed the poor woman. "Ef you capters them men erginst ther will, they'll git away ergin — *sho!* Let 'im go long! He ain't paid me a cent or a ration of meat an' meal sence he was ma'ied. Anyhow," she proudly added, "*M'ay Ann is mated!* Folks can't fling it up to 'er now as she's a ole maid," — which proves that maternal ambitions are peculiar to no condition of life.

Looking back, and living over again these stern times, it seems to me little short of a miracle that we actually did exist upon the slender portion of food allotted us. We could rarely see, from one day to another, just how we were to be fed. "Give us this day our daily bread"—this petition was our sole reliance. And as surely as the day would come, "He that doth the ravens feed, Yea, providently caters for the sparrow," would prove to us that we were of more value in His sight than many sparrows.

General Lee passed my door every Sunday morning on his way to a little wooden chapel nearer his quarters than St. Paul's Church. I have a picture of him in my memory, in his faded gray overcoat and slouch hat, bending his head before the sleet on stormy mornings. Sometimes his cousin, Mrs. Banister, could find herself warranted by circumstances to invite him to dine with her. Once she received from a country friend a present of a turkey, and General Lee consented to share it with her. She helped him at dinner to a moderate portion, for there was only one turkey—like Charles Lamb's hare—and many friends! Mrs. Banister observed the general laying on one side of his plate part of his share of the turkey, and she regretted his loss of appetite. "Madam," he explained, "Colonel Taylor is not well, and I should be glad to be permitted to take this to him."

After an unusually mild season, John bethought himself of the fishes in the pond and streams, but not a fishhook was for sale in Richmond or Petersburg. He contrived, out of a cunning arrangement of pins, to make hooks, and sallied forth with my boys. But the water was too cold, or the fish had been driven down-stream by the firing. The usual resource of the sportsman with an empty creel—a visit to the fishmonger—was quite out of the question. There was no fishmonger any more.

Under these circumstances you may imagine my sensation at receiving the following note:

"MY DEAR MRS. PRYOR: General Lee has been honored by a visit from the Hon. Thomas Connolly, Irish M.P. from Donegal.

"He ventures to request you will have the kindness to give Mr. Connolly a room in your cottage, if this can be done without inconvenience to yourself."

Certainly I could give Mr. Connolly a room; but just as certainly I could not feed him! The messenger who brought me the note hastily reassured me. He had been instructed to say that Mr. Connolly would mess with General Lee. I turned Mr. Connolly's room over to John, who soon became devoted to his service. The M.P. proved a most agreeable guest, a fine-looking Irish gentleman with an irresistibly humorous, cheery fund of talk. He often dropped in at our biscuit toasting, and assured us that we were better provided than the commander-in-chief.

"You should have seen 'Uncle Robert's' dinner to-day, madam! He had two biscuits, and he gave me one."

Another time Mr. Connolly was in high feather.

"We had a glorious dinner to-day! Somebody sent 'Uncle Robert' a box of sardines."

General Lee, however, was not forgotten. On fine mornings quite a procession of little negroes, in every phase of raggedness, used to pass my door, each one bearing a present from the farmers' wives of buttermilk in a tin pail for General Lee. The army was threatened with scurvy, and buttermilk, hominy, and every vegetable that could be obtained was sent to the hospital.

Mr. Connolly interested himself in my boys' Latin studies.

"I am going home," he said, "and tell the English women what I have seen here: two boys reading Caesar while the shells are thundering, and their mother looking on without fear."

"I am too busy keeping the wolf from my door," I told him, "to concern myself with the thunderbolts."

The wolf was no longer at the door! He had entered and had taken up his abode at the fireside. Besides what I could earn with my needle, I had only my father's army ration to rely upon. My faithful John foraged right and left, and I had reason to doubt the wisdom of inquiring too closely as to the source of an occasional half-dozen eggs or small bag of corn. This last he would pound on a wooden block for hominy. Meal was greatly prized for the reason that wholesomer bread could be made of it than of wheaten flour, — meal was no longer procurable, but we were never altogether without flour. As I have said, we might occasionally purchase for five dollars the head of a bullock from the commissary, every other part of the animal being available for army rations. By self-denial on our own part we fondly hoped we could support our army and at last win our cause. We were not, at the time, fully aware of the true state of things in the army. Our men were so depleted from starvation that the most trifling wound would end fatally. Gangrene would supervene, and then nothing could be done to prevent death. Long before this time, at Vicksburg, Admiral Porter found that many a dead soldier's haversack yielded nothing but a handful of parched corn. *We* were now enduring a sterner siege. The month of January brought us sleet and storm. Our famine grew sterner every day. Seasons of bitter cold weather would find us without wood to burn, and we had no other fuel. I commenced cutting down the choice fruit trees in the grounds, — and General Wilcox managed to send me a load of rails from a fence, hitherto spared by the soldiers. Poor little Rose could yield only one cupful of milk, so small was her ration; but we never thought of turning the faithful animal into beef. The officers in my yard spared her something every day from the food of their horses.

The days were so dark and cheerless, the news from the armies at a distance so discouraging, it was hard to preserve a cheerful demeanor for the sake of the family. And now began the alarming tidings, every morning, of the desertions during the night. General Wilcox wondered how long his brigade would hold together at the rate of fifty desertions every twenty-four hours!

The common soldier had enlisted, not to establish the right of secession, not for love of the slave,—he had no slaves,—but simply to resist the invasion of the South by the North, simply to prevent subjugation. The soldier of the rank and file was not always intellectual or cultivated. He cared little for politics, less for slavery. He did care, however, for his own soil, his own little farm, his own humble home, and he was willing to fight to drive the invader from it. Lincoln's Emancipation Proclamation did not stimulate him in the least. The negro, free or slave, was of no consequence to him. His quarrel was a sectional one, and he fought for his section.

In any war the masses rarely trouble themselves about the merits of the quarrel. Their pugnacity and courage are aroused and stimulated by the enthusiasm of their comrades or by their own personal wrongs and perils.

Now, in January, 1865, the common soldier perceived that the cause was lost. He could read its doom in the famine around him, in the faces of his officers, in tidings from abroad. His wife and children were suffering. His duty was now to them; so he stole away in the darkness, and in infinite danger and difficulty found his way back to his own fireside. He deserted, but not to the enemy.

But what shall we say of the soldier who remained unflinching at his post *knowing* the cause was lost for which he was called to meet death? Heroism can attain no loftier height than this. Very few of the intelligent men of our army had the slightest hope, at the end, of our success. Some, like Mr. William C. Rives, had none at the beginning.

One night all these things weighed more heavily

than usual upon me, — the picket firing, the famine, the military executions, the dear one "sick and in prison." I sighed audibly, and my son Theodorick, who slept near me, asked the cause, adding, "Why can you not sleep, dear mother?"

"Suppose," I replied, "you repeat something for me."

He at once commenced, "Tell me not in mournful numbers " — and repeated the "Psalm of Life." I did not sleep; those were brave words, but not strong enough for the situation.

He paused, and presently his young voice broke the stillness:

"Bless the Lord, O my soul, and all that is within me, bless His holy name" — going on to the end of the beautiful psalm of adoration and faith which nineteen centuries have decreed to be in very truth a Psalm of Life.

That General Lee was acutely sensible of our condition was proved by an interview with General Gordon. Before daylight, on the 2nd of March, General Lee sent for General Gordon, who was with his command at a distant part of the line. Upon arriving, General Gordon was much affected by seeing General Lee standing at the mantel in his room, his head bowed on his folded arms. The room was dimly lighted by a single lamp, and a smouldering fire was dying on the hearth. The night was cold, and General Lee's room chill and cheerless.

"I have sent for you, General Gordon," said General Lee, with a dejected voice and manner, "to make known to you the condition of our affairs and consult with you as to what we had best do. I have here reports sent in from my officers to-night. I find I have under my command, of all arms, hardly forty-five thousand men. These men are starving. They are already so weakened as to be hardly efficient. Many of them have become desperate, reckless, and disorderly as they have never been before.

"It is difficult to control men who are suffering for food. They are breaking open mills, barns, and stores in search of it. Almost crazed from hunger, they are deserting in large numbers and going home. My horses are in equally bad condition. The supply of horses in the country is exhausted. It has come to be just as bad for me to have a horse killed as a man. I cannot remount a cavalryman whose horse dies. General Grant can mount ten thousand men in ten days and move round your flank. If he were to send me word to-morrow that I might move out unmolested, I have not enough horses to move my artillery. He is not likely to send me any such message, although he sent me word yesterday that he knew what I had for breakfast every morning. I sent him word I did not think that this could be so, for if he did he would surely send me something better.

"But now let us look at the figures. As I said, I have forty-five thousand starving men. Hancock has eighteen thousand at Winchester. To oppose him I have not a single vidette. Sheridan, with his terrible cavalry, has marched unmolested and unopposed along the James, cutting the railroads and the canal. Thomas is coming from Knoxville with thirty thousand well-equipped troops, and I have, to oppose him, not more than three thousand in all. Sherman is in North Carolina with sixty-five thousand men. So I have forty-five thousand poor fellows in bad condition opposed to one hundred and sixty thousand strong and confident men. These forces added to General Grant's make over a quarter of a million. To prevent them all from uniting to my destruction, and adding Johnston's and Beauregard's men, I can oppose only sixty thousand men. They are growing weaker every day. Their sufferings are terrible and exhausting. My horses are broken down and impotent. General Grant may press around our flank any day and cut off our supplies."

As a result of this conference General Lee went to Richmond to make one more effort to induce our government to treat for peace. It was on his return from an utterly fruitless errand that he said:

"I am a soldier! It is my duty to obey orders;" and the final disastrous battles were fought.

It touches me to know now that it was after this that my beloved commander found heart to turn aside and bring me comfort. No one knew better than he all I had endeavored and endured, and my heart blesses his memory for its own sake. At this tremendous moment, when he had returned from his fruitless mission to Richmond, when the attack on Fort Steadman was impending, when his slender line was confronted by Grant's ever increasing host, stretching twenty miles, when the men were so starved, so emaciated, that the smallest wound meant death, when his own personal privations were beyond imagination, General Lee could spend half an hour for my consolation and encouragement.

Cottage Farm being on the road between head-quarters and Fort Gregg, — the fortification which held General Grant in check at that point, — I saw General Lee almost daily going to this work or to Battery 45.

I was, as was my custom, sewing in my little parlor one morning, about the middle of March, when an orderly entered, saying:

"General Lee wishes to make his respects to Mrs. Pryor." The general was immediately behind him. His face was lighted with the anticipation of telling me his good news. With the high-bred courtesy and kindness which always distinguished his manner, he asked kindly after my welfare, and taking my little girl in his arms, began gently to break his news to me:

"How long, madam, was General Pryor with me before he had a furlough?"

"He never had one, I think," I answered.

"Well, did I not take good care of him until we camped here so close to you?"

"Certainly," I said, puzzled to know the drift of these preliminaries.

"I sent him home to you, I remember," he continued, "for a day or two, and you let the Yankees catch him. Now he is coming back to be with you again on parole until he is exchanged. You must take better care of him in future."

I was too much overcome to do more than stammer a few words of thanks.

Presently he added, "What are you going to say when I tell the general that in all this winter you have never once been to see me?"

"Oh, General Lee," I answered, "I had too much mercy to join in your buttermilk persecution!"

"Persecution!" he said; "such things keep us alive! Last night, when I reached my headquarters, I found a card on my table with a hyacinth pinned to it, and these words: 'For General Lee, with a kiss!' Now," he added, tapping his breast, "I have here my hyacinth and my card—*and I mean to find my kiss!*"

He was amused by the earnest eyes of my little girl, as she gazed into his face.

"They have a wonderful liking for soldiers," he said. "I knew one little girl to give up all her pretty curls willingly that she might look like Custis! 'They *might* cut my hair like Custis's,' she said. Custis! whose shaven head does not improve him in any eyes but hers."

His manner was the perfection of repose and simplicity. As he talked with me, I remembered that I had heard of this singular calmness. Even at Gettysburg and at the explosion of the crater he had evinced no agitation or dismay. I did not know then, as I do now, that nothing had ever approached the anguish of this moment, when he had come to say an encouraging and cheering word to me, after abandoning all hope of the success of the cause.

After talking awhile and sending a kind message to my husband, to greet him on his return, he rose, walked to the window, and looked over the fields,— the fields through which, not many days afterward, he dug his last trenches!

I was moved to say, "You only, General, can tell me if it is worth my while to put the ploughshare into those fields."

"Plant your seeds, madam," he replied; sadly adding, after a moment, "The doing it will be some reward."

I was answered. I thought then he had little hope. I now know he had none.

He had already, as we have seen, remonstrated against further resistance — against the useless shedding of blood. His protest had been unheeded. It remained for him now to gather his forces for endurance to the end.

Twenty days afterward his headquarters were in ashes; he had led his famished army across the Appomattox, and telling them they had done their duty and had nothing to regret, he had bidden them farewell forever.

Chapter LXXII: Evacuation of Richmond — Burning of the City

From *In Richmond During the War* (1867)

Sallie A. Brock Putnam

THE morning of the 2nd of April, 1865, dawned brightly over the capital of the Southern Confederacy. A soft haze rested over the city, but above that, the sun shone with the warm pleasant radiance of early spring. The sky was cloudless. No sound disturbed the stillness of the Sabbath morn, save the subdued murmur of the river, and the cheerful music of the church bells. The long familiar tumult of war broke not upon the sacred calmness of the day. Around the War Department, and the Post Office, news gatherers were assembled for the latest tidings, but nothing was bruited that deterred the masses from seeking their accustomed places in the temples of the living God. At St. Paul's church the usual congregation was in attendance. President Davis occupied his pew.

It was again the regular monthly return for the celebration of the sacrament of the Lord's Supper. The services were progressing as usual, no agitation nor disturbance withdrew the thoughts from holy contemplation, when a messenger was observed to make his way up the aisle, and to place in the hands of the President a sealed package. Mr. Davis arose, and was noticed to walk rather unsteadily out of the church. An uneasy whisper ran through the congregation, and intuitively they seemed possessed of the dreadful secret of the sealed dispatch—the unhappy condition or General Lee's army and the necessity for evacuating Richmond. The dispatch stated that this was inevitable unless his lines could be reformed before eight o'clock that evening.

At the Second Presbyterian Church, Dr. Hoge, who had received information of the dire calamity impending over us, told his congregation of our situation, and the probability that never again would they meet there for worship, and in the thrilling eloquence of which he is so truly the master, bade them farewell.

The direful tidings spread with the swiftness of electricity. From lip to lip, from men, women, children and servants, the news was bandied, but many received it at first, as only a "Sunday sensation rumor." Friend looked into the face of friend to meet only an expression of incredulity; but later in the day, as the truth, stark and appalling, confronted us, the answering look was that of stony, calm despair. Late in the afternoon the signs of evacuation became obvious to even the most incredulous. Wagons were driven furiously through the streets, to the different departments, where they received as freight, the archives of the government, and carried them to the Danville Depot, to be here conveyed away by railroad.

Thousands of the citizens determined to evacuate the city with the government. Vehicles commanded any price in any currency possessed by the individual desiring to escape from the doomed capital. The streets were filled with excited crowds hurrying to the different avenues for transportation, intermingled with porters carrying huge loads, and wagons piled up with incongruous heaps of baggage, of all sorts and descriptions. The banks were all open, and depositors were busily and anxiously collecting their specie deposits, and directors were as busily engaged in getting off their bullion. Millions of dollars of paper money, both State and Confederate, were carried to the Capitol Square and buried.

Night came on, but with it no sleep for human eyes in Richmond. Confusion worse confounded reigned, and grim terror spread in wild contagion. The City Council met, and ordered the destruction of all spirituous liquors, fearing lest, in the excitement, there would be temptation to drink, and thus render our situation still more terrible. In the gutters ran a stream of whiskey, and its fumes filled and impregnated the air. After nightfall Richmond was ruled by the mob. In the principal business section of the city they surged in one black mass from store to store, breaking them open, robbing them, and in some instances (it is said) applying the torch to them.

In the alarm and terror, the guards of the State Penitentiary fled from their posts, and numbers of the lawless and desperate villains incarcerated there, for crimes of every grade and hue, after setting fire to the workshops, made good the opportunity for escape, and donning garments stolen wherever they could get them, in exchange for their prison livery, roamed over the city like fierce, ferocious beasts. No human tongue, no pen, however gifted, can give an adequate description of the events of that awful night.

While these fearful scenes were being enacted on the streets, in-doors there was scarcely less excitement and confusion. Into every house terror penetrated. Ladies were busily engaged in collecting and secreting all the valuables possessed by them, together with cherished correspondence, yet they found time and presence of mind to prepare a few comforts for friends forced to depart with the army or the government. Few tears were shed; there was no time for weakness or sentiment. The grief was too deep, the agony too terrible to find vent through the ordinary channels of distress. Fathers, husbands, brothers and friends clasped their loved ones to their bosoms in convulsive and agonized embraces, and bade an adieu, oh, how heart-rending!* perhaps, thought many of them, forever.

---

* At eleven o'clock on that night, Colonel ——,on General ——'s staff, came into thecity and was married. In a few moments he left his bride in the terrible uncertainty of ever again meeting.

At midnight the train on the Danville Railroad bore off the officers of the Government, and at the same hour many persons made their escape on the canal packets, and fled in the direction of Lynchburg.

But a still more terrible element was destined to appear and add to the horrors of the scene. From some authority—it seems uncertain what—an order had been issued to fire the four principal tobacco warehouses. They were so situated as to jeopardize the entire commercial portion of Richmond. At a late hour of the night, Mayor Mayo had dispatched, by a committee of citizens, a remonstrance against this reckless military order. But in the mad excitement of the moment the protest was unheeded. The torch was applied, and the helpless citizens were left to witness the destruction of their property. The rams in the James River were blown up. The "Richmond," the "Virginia" No. 2 and the "Beaufort" were all scattered in fiery fragments to the four winds of heaven. The noise of these explosions, which occurred as the first grey streaks of dawn broke over Richmond, was like that or a hundred cannon at one time. The very foundations of the city were shaken; windows were shattered more than two miles from where these gunboats were exploded, and the frightened inhabitants imagined that the place was being furiously bombarded. The "Patrick Henry," a receiving-ship, was scuttled, and all the shipping at the wharves was fired except the flag-of-truce steamer "Allison."

As the sun rose on Richmond, such a spectacle

was presented as can never be forgotten by those who witnessed it. To speed destruction, some malicious and foolish individuals had cut the hose in the city. The fire was progressing with fearful rapidity. The roaring, the hissing, and the crackling of the flames were heard above the shouting and confusion of the immense crowd of plunderers who were moving amid the dense smoke like demons, pushing, rioting and swaying with their burdens to make a passage to the open air. From the lower portion of the city, near the river, dense black clouds of smoke arose as a pall of crape to hide the ravages of the devouring flames, which lifted their red tongues and leaped from building to building as if possessed of demoniac instinct, and intent upon wholesale destruction. All the railroad bridges, and Mayo's Bridge, that crossed the James River and connected with Manchester, on the opposite side, were in flames.

The most remarkable scenes, however, were said to have occurred at the commissary depot. Hundreds of Government wagons were loaded with bacon, flour, and whiskey, and driven off in hot haste to join the retreating army. In a dense throng around the depot stood hundreds of men, women and children, black and white, provided with anything in which they could carry away provisions, awaiting the opening of the doors to rush in and help themselves. A cascade of whiskey streamed from the windows. About sunrise the doors were thrown open to the populace, and with a rush that seemed almost sufficient to bear off the building itself, they soon swept away all that remained of the Confederate commissariat of Richmond.

By this time the flames had been applied to or had reached the arsenal, in which several hundred car loads of loaded shell were left. At every moment the most terrific explosions were sending forth their awful reverberations, and gave us the idea of a general bombardment. All the horrors of the final conflagration, when the earth shall be wrapped in flames and melt with fervent heat, were, it seemed to us, prefigured in our capital.

At an early hour in the morning, the Mayor of the city, to whom it had been resigned by the military commander, proceeded to the lines of the enemy and surrendered it to General Godfrey Weitzel, who had been left by General Ord, when he withdrew one-half of his division to the lines investing Petersburg, to receive the surrender of Richmond.

As early as eight o'clock in the morning, while the mob held possession of Main street, and were busily helping themselves to the contents of the dry goods stores and other shops in that portion of the city, and while a few of our cavalry were still to be seen here and there in the upper portions, a cry was raised: "The Yankees! The Yankees are coming!" Major A. H. Stevens, of the Fourth Massachusetts Cavalry, and Major E. E. Graves, of his staff, with forty cavalry, rode steadily into the city, proceeded directly to the Capitol, and planted once more the "Stars and Stripes" — the ensign of our subjugation — on that ancient edifice. As its folds were given to the breeze, while still we heard the roaring, hissing, crackling flames, the explosions of the shells and the shouting of the multitude, the strains of an old, familiar tune floated upon the air — a tune that, in days gone by, was wont to awaken a thrill of patriotism. But now only the most bitter and crushing recollections awoke within us, as upon our quickened hearing fell the strains of "The Star Spangled Banner." For us it was a requiem for buried hopes.

As the day advanced, Weitzel's troops poured through the city. Long lines of negro calvary swept by the Exchange Hotel, brandishing their swords and uttering savage cheers, replied to by the shouts of those of their own color, who were trudging along under loads of plunder, laughing and exulting over the prizes they had secured from the wreck of the stores, rather than rejoicing at the more precious prize of freedom which had been won for them. On passed the colored troops, singing, "John Brown's body is mouldering in the grave," etc.

By one o'clock in the day, the confusion reached its height. As soon as the Federal troops reached the city they were set to work by the officers to arrest the progress of the fire. By this time a wind had risen from the south, and seemed likely to carry the surging flames all over the northwestern portion of the city. The most strenuous efforts were made to prevent this, and the grateful thanks of the people of Richmond are due to General Weitzel and other officers for their energetic measures to save the city from entire destruction.

The Capitol Square now presented a novel appearance. On the south, east, and west of its lower half, it was bounded by burning buildings. The flames bursting from the windows, and rising from the roofs, were proclaiming in one wild roar their work of destruction. Myriads of sparks, borne upward by the current of hot air, were brightening and breaking in the dense smoke above. On the sward of the Square, fresh with the emerald green of early spring, thousands of wretched creatures, who had been driven from their dwellings by the devouring flames, were congregated. Fathers and mothers, and weeping, frightened children sought this open space for a breath of fresh air. But here, even, it was almost as hot as a furnace. Intermingled with these miserable beings were the Federal troops in their garish uniform, representing almost every nation on the continent of Europe, and thousands of the *Corps d'Afrique*. All along on the north side of the Square were tethered the horses of the Federal cavalry, while, dotted about, were seen the white tents of the sutlers, in which there were temptingly displayed canned fruits and meats, crackers, cheese, etc.

The roaring, crackling and hissing of the flames, the bursting of shells at the Confederate Arsenal, the sounds of instruments or martial music, the neighing of the horses, the shoutings of the multitude, in which could be distinctly distinguished the coarse, wild voices of the negroes, gave an idea of an the horrors of Pandemonium. Above all this scene of terror, hung a black shroud of smoke through which the sun shone with a lurid angry glare like an immense ball of blood that emitted sullen rays of light, as if loth to shine over a scene so appalling.

Remembering the unhappy fate of the citizens of Columbia and other cities of the South, and momentarily expecting pillage, and other evils incidental to the sacking of a city, great numbers of ladies sought the proper military authorities and were furnished with safeguards for the protection of themselves and their homes. These were willingly and generously furnished, and no scene of violence is remembered to have been committed by the troops which occupied Richmond.

Throughout the entire day, those who had enriched themselves by plundering the stores were busy in conveying off their goods. Laughing and jesting negroes tugged along with every conceivable description of merchandise, and many an astute shopkeeper from questionable quarters of Richmond thus added greatly to his former stock.

The sun had set upon this terrible day before the awful reverberations of exploding shells at the arsenal ceased to be heard over Richmond. The evening came on. A deathlike quiet pervaded the late heaving and tumultuous city, broken only by the murmuring waters of the river. Night drew her sable mantle over the mutilated remains of our beautiful capital, and we locked, and bolted, and barred our doors; but sleep had fled our eyelids. All night long we kept a fearful vigil, and listened with beating heart and quickened ears for the faintest sound that might indicate the development of other and more terrible phases of horror. But from all these we were mercifully and providentially spared.

We will just here notice the range and extent of the fire which had in the afternoon literally burned itself out. From an authentic account we copy at length:

"It had consumed the very heart of the city. A surveyor could scarcely have designated the business portion of the city more exactly than did the boundaries of the fire. Commencing at the Shockoe warehouse the fire radiated front and rear, and on two wings, burning down to, but not destroying, the store No. 77 Main street, south side, halfway between Fourteenth and Fifteenth Streets, and back to the river through Cary and all the intermediate streets. Westward on Main the fire was stayed on Ninth Street, sweeping back to the river. On the north side of Main, the flames were stayed between Thirteenth and Fourteenth, streets. From this point the flames raged on the north side of Main up to Eighth Street, and back to Bank Street.

"Among some of the most prominent of the buildings destroyed were the Bank of Richmond, Traders' Bank, Bank of the Commonwealth, Bank of Virginia, Farmers' Bank, ten of the banking houses, the American Hotel, the Columbian Hotel, the Enquirer building, on Twelfth street, the Dispatch office and job-rooms, corner of Thirteenth and Main Streets, all that block of buildings known as Belvin's Block, the Examiner office, engine and machinery rooms, the Confederate Post Office Department building, the State Court House, a fine old building on the Capitol Square at its Franklin Street entrance, the Mechanics' Institute, vacated by the Confederate War Department, and all the buildings on that Square up to Eighth Street, and back to Main Street, the Confederate Arsenal, and the Laboratory on Seventh Street.

"The streets were crowded with furniture and every description of wares, dashed down and trampled in the mud, or burned where it lay. All the government stores were thrown open, and what could not be gotten off by the government was left to the people.

"Next to the river the destruction of property was fearfully complete. The Danville and Petersburg Railroad depots, and the buildings and shedding attached, for the distance of half-a-mile from the north side of Main Street to the river, and between Eighth and Fifteenth Streets, embracing upwards of twenty blocks, presented one waste of smoking ruins, blackened walls, and solitary chimneys."

Except the great fire in New York, in 1837, there is said never to have been so extensive a conflagration on this continent as the burning of Richmond on that memorable day.

Upon reaching the city, General Weitzel established his headquarters in the Hall of the State Capitol, previously occupied by the Virginia House of Delegates. He immediately issued an order for the restoration of quiet, and intended to allay the fears and restore confidence and tranquility to the minds of the inhabitants, General Shepley was appointed Military Commander of Richmond, and Lieutenant-Colonel Fred L. Manning was made acting Provost Marshal.

General Shepley issued an order which protected the citizens from insult and depredation by the Federal soldiers, and which also included a morbidly sensitive clause in deprecation of insult to the "flag," calculated rather to excite the derision than the indignation of the conquered inhabitants.

The scenes of this day give rise to many reflections, the most of which are too deeply painful to dwell upon. The spirit of extortion, the wicked and inordinate greed of mammon which sometimes overclouds and overules all the nobler instincts of humanity, are strikingly illustrated by a single incident in this connection. A lady passed up Franklin Street early on the morning of the 3rd of April, and held in her hand a small phial in which there was about a table spoonful of paregoric. "This," said she, "I have just purchased on Main Street, at ——'s drug store. Richmond is in flames, and yet for this spoonful of medicine for a sick servant I had to pay five dollars."

An hour had not passed when the fire consumed the establishment of the extortionate vender of drugs. This incident points a moral which all can apply. Riches take to themselves wings, and in a moment least expected elude our grasp. Many who shirked the conscription, who made unworthy use of exemption bills, for the purpose of heaping up and watching their ill-gotten treasures, saw them in a single hour reduced to ashes and made the sport of the winds of heaven. Truly man knoweth not what a day may bring forth.

The principal pillar that sustained the Confederate fabric had been overthrown, the chief corner-stone had been loosened and pushed from its place, and the crumbling of the entire edifice to a ruined and shapeless mass seemed to us but a question of time.

POETRY

Virginia's Message to the Southern States

From *Southern Poems of the War* (1867)

YOU dared not think I'd never come;
You could not doubt your Mother,
If traitorous chains had crushed *my form,*

My soul with yours had hovered.
Yes, children, I have come;
We'll stand together, we'll be one,
Brave dangers, death, and wars begun!
Where should this struggle work and end?
Where should this conflict be?
Where should we all our rights defend,

And gain our liberty?
Upon *my* soil your swords you'll wield,
Upon *my* soil your homes you'll shield,
And on *my* soil your foes *shall* yield!

Where, but on my mountains' heights,
And on my rivers' banks,
Where, but 'neath *ray* heavens' lights,

And in my children's camps,
Shall all the blood be shed,
In streams of living red,
And all our foes be dead?

Then, soldiers brave, come forth,
Ye sons of *noble mothers!* They'll chide you if you're loth
And yield your homes to others. Mothers! send them,
    then, without a tear Bid
them go, and make all earth revere *Their country's honor
    and a soldier's bier!*

—Anonymous

Heart Victories, By a Soldier's Wife

From *Southern Poems of the War* (1867)

THERE'S not a stately hall,
There's not a cottage fair, that proudly stands on
    Southern soil,
    Or softly nestles there, But in its peaceful walls
With wealth or comfort blessed, A stormy battle fierce
    hath raged
    In gentle woman's breast.
There Love, the true, the brave,
The beautiful, the strong, Wrestles with Duty, gaunt
    and stern,
Wrestles and struggles long. He falls—no more again
His giant foe to meet, Bleeding at every opening vein,
Love falls at Duty's feet.
Daughter of the South,
    No victor's crown be thine, Not thine, upon the
        tented field
    In martial pomp to shine; But with unfaltering
        trust
    In Him who rules on high,
To deck thy loved ones for the fray,
And send them forth to die.

—Anonymous

A Mother's Prayer

From *Southern Poems of the War* (1867)

[*The lady who wrote the following was thrown into a state of great agitation and alarm from the occurrences of the terrible Friday, April 19th, 1861. Not being able to sleep, she expressed her feelings in writing the following prayer. This statement is made by the person in whose hands she placed the original manuscript, and who is one of the family. E.P.*]

GOD of nations, God of might,
In the stillness of the night,
At Thy footstool low I bow
Hear me, hear me, hear me now.

All without is dark and drear,
All within is doubt and fear;
Where for refuge can I flee,
God of Hosts, if not to Thee!

What fierce scourging, Judge of all,
Must upon my country fall?
Must we o'er this land so fair
Witness carnage and despair?

All withdrawn Thy fav'ring light,
All our noonday turn'd to night.
Oh, if I, in anguish bow'd,
May not see behind the cloud,
May not have one gleam to dart
Through the gloom that shrouds my heart,
From its depths, where thou canst see,
In the dust I cry to Thee.

We have sinned, oh God of might,
Sinned, rebellious in Thy sight;

Pride and wrath are o'er the land,
But, avenger, stay Thine hand;
For our children smiling here,
For our little ones so dear,
Stay Thy judgment swift and sure:
Stay it, God, for these are pure.

By the child whose feeble cry
From the desert rose on high,
Bringing to the mother there
Angel cheer in her despair!
By the babe that Thou didst save
From the Nile's engulfing wave
By the children He did press
To His breast in soft caress—
And the loud Hosannah song
Rising from the infant throng
Save us, save us, spare Thine hand;
For the children, save the land.

Dark, still dark, no light I trace,
Hast Thou turned away Thy face?
Must we walk this fiery path,
Scowl'd upon by direful wrath?

Must we to the dust go down
Blasted by Thy hopeless frown?
If so, Father, we obey,
But for the young I still would pray.

For the young I make my moan,
Such as these, my own, my own;
These, my boys in rosy rest,
This, the babe upon my breast,
Little dreaming as they sleep
Why their mother wakes to weep
Oh! let me but feel the rod,
Spare them, spare them, Oh my God!

And for all so passion-tossed,
All this people ruined, lost;
Forgetting now their ancient trust,
Tramping all they loved in dust
Still I cry, for only Thou
Canst control and save them now.

By the mercy Thou didst show
To Thy people long ago,
When by Thee released, restored,
They like us forgot Thee, Lord
By the prayer of Him who died,
By His love, the crucified,
And the tears He wept o'er them
Wept o'er doomed Jerusalem;
Oh! forgive, forgive us, Lord,
Let Thy pity be restored;
Say again, if tis Thy will,
To these billows Peace, Be Still!

—*Mrs. Makgabet Figoot*

The Battle Eve

From *The Southern Amaranth* (1869)

I SEE the broad, red, setting sun
Sink slowly down the sky;
I see, amid the cloud-built tents,
His blood-red standard fly;
And meek, meanwhile, the pallid moon
Looks from her place on high.

Oh, setting sun, awhile delay!
Longer on sea and shore;
For thousand eyes now gaze on thee,
That shall not see thee more;
A thousand hearts beat proudly now,
Whose race, like thine, is o'er!

Oh, ghastly moon! Thy pallid ray
On paler brows shall lie!
On many a torn and bleeding heart,
On many a glazing eye;
And breaking hearts shall live to mourn,
For whom 'twere bliss to die!

—*Susan Archer Tally*

The Soldier's Grave

From *Southern Poems of the War* (1867)

'TIS where no chisel's tracing tells
The humble sleeper's name,
No storied marble proudly swells

The measure of his fame.
Nor while the pensive moonbeams sleep
Upon the dim blue wave,
Do mourning kindred come to weep

Beside the *soldier's grave*.
But, poised upon her gleaming wings,
The beauteous summer bird,

In sweet and melting strains to sing
His requiem, is heard.

And oft as Spring her garland weaves,
There blooms her dewy rose,

And autumn strews her yellow leaves
Above his deep repose.

So true is Nature to his tomb,
So true I almost crave,
While musing on the soldier's doom,

To fill a soldier's grave.

—Anonymous

Mumford's Grave

From *The Southern Amaranth* (1869)

"SLEEP knits up the raveled sleeve of care,"
They say. O, would it knit up mine, and not
Leave this suffering heart of mine so bare.
A nightmare sits upon me, ever cold and grim,
And wherefore, the horrid vision of a murdered Love
A set of dastard cowards; for what? Listen,
Gentle reader. A mighty foe besieged a city
Filled with non-combatants, helpless women and
    children,
And ere the city had surrendered, hoisted a hated
Symbol, of Stars and Stripes, a strip or rag,
Perchance, it will be, must be.
He, the murdered man, he tore it down amid
A shower of shot and shell—what cared he for his life?
"Shall it be said they hoisted up their flag before
The city had surrendered? Never, I will tear it down
    or die!"
He died as a Southern man should and can die—
For the honor of his country—a Martyr.
He sleeps, a sleep that knows no waking,
In a bright and joyous world, where sits a judge
The avenger of unjust and murderous deeds.
But there is one who lives, and breathes and moves,
And does he sleep? Perchance to dream
Of goblins, scaffolds, a father pleading
For his life, a pale face craving pardon
For the father of her children—such dreams!
And do they leave no weight upon him in his
Waking hours? Let conscience answer.

—Lines By His Widow

The Jacket of Gray: To Those Who Wore It

From *Southern Poems of the War* (1867)

FOLD it up carefully, lay it aside,
Tenderly touch it, look on it with pride,
For dear must it be to our hearts evermore,
The jacket of gray our loved soldier boy wore.

Can we ever forget when he joined the brave band,
Who rose in defense of dear Southern land;
And in his bright youth hurried on to the fray,
How proudly he donn'd it, the jacket of gray!

His fond mother blessed him and looked up above,
Commending to Heaven the child of her love,
What anguish was hers, mortal tongue may not say,
When he passed from her sight in the jacket of gray.

But her country had called him, she would not repine,
Tho' costly the sacrifice placed on its shrine;
Her heart's dearest hopes on its altar she lay,
When she sent out her boy, in his jacket of gray!

Months passed, and War's thunders rolled over the land,
Unsheathed was the sword and lighted the brand;
We heard in the distance the noise of the fray,
And prayed for our boy, in the jacket of gray.

Ah! vain all, — all vain were our prayers and our tears,
The glad shout of victory rang in our ears;
But our treasured one on the cold battle-field lay,
While the life blood oozed out on the jacket of gray.

Fold it up carefully, lay it aside,
Tenderly touch it, look on it with pride;
For dear must it be to our hearts evermore,
The jacket of gray our loved soldier boy wore.

His young comrades found him and tenderly bore
His cold lifeless form to his home by the shore;
Oh! dark were our hearts on that terrible day
When we saw our dead boy in the jacket of gray.

Ah! spotted, and tattered, and stained now with gore,
Was the garment which once he so gracefully wore;
We bitterly wept as we took it away,
And replaced with death's white robes the jacket of gray.

We laid him to rest in his cold narrow bed,
And graved on the marble we placed o'er his head,
As the proudest of tributes our sad hearts could pay,
"He never disgraced the dear jacket of gray."

Then fold it up carefully, lay it aside,
Tenderly touch it, look on it with pride;
For dear must it be to our hearts evermore,
The jacket of gray our loved soldier boy wore.

—*Mrs. C. A. Ball*

Virginia

From *Beechenbrook:A Rhyme of the War and Other Civil War Poems* (1866)

GRANDLY then fillest the world's eye to-day,

> My proud Virginia! When the gage was thrown—
> The deadly gage of battle—thou, alone,

Strong in thy self-control, didst stoop to lay

The olive-branch thereon, and calmly pray

> We might have peace; the rather. When the foe
> Turned scornfully upon thee,—bade thee go,

And whistled up his war-hounds, then—the way

> Of duty full before thee,—thou didst spring
> Into the centre of the martial ring—

Thy brave blood boiling, and thy glorious eye,

> Shot with heroic fire, and swear to claim
> Sublimest victory in God's own name,—

Or, wrapped in robes of martyrdom,—to die!

—Margaret J. Preston

Virginia

From *Virginia and Other Poems* (1881)

PRELUDE

AS timid bird that fears to soar too high,
Yet dares not thwart the power that bids her rise;
As uttering truths he knows can never die,
The slow-tongued prophet whom all hearts despise,
Keeps steadfast gaze where men can nothing see,
And speaks because he must — I sing of thee.

As sailor, seeking some small isle, beholds
Rich, boundless lands as from the waters called;
As Newton, searching earth's great law, unfolds
That of a universe, and shrinks appalled;
So do I view thee, Land of hope and dream,
Lost in the mighty grandeur of my theme,

Ah, poor thou art indeed, if none but me
Remain of-all thou hadst to sing of thee.

And yet I am not all unworthy; none
Of those who did for thee lie down and die,
E'er honored, worshipped thee through storm and sun,
With truer, deeper reverence than I.
None at thy call for aid would quicker spring,
None in thy piteous weakness closer cling.

I love thy fields, and skies, and forests deep,
Thy rivers, and thy mountains, glens, and vales;
I love the very mists that o'er thee creep,
The winds that compass thee with shrieks and wails.
And more, the hearts where Honor still survives,
And still thy grand old spirit, chafing, lives.

If, as is said, the poet in his lay
Weaveth his life-blood that his song may live,
Surely these lines shall in some memory stay,
For, with each word, part of myself I give;
And thought must wake to thought, part fit to part,
Soul breathe to soul, and heart respond to heart.

As one of slow and stammering speech is heard
In gentle patience for the truth he brings, —
Not for some brilliant and high-sounding word, —
So, though unmusical the voice that sings,
My theme shall lend a value to my song
Arid turn its harsh to sweet, its weak to strong.

And if, perchance, the power to win and wear
Earth's fame and horror should be found in me,
As olden knight brought to his lady fair
His trophies, I would give the whole to thee,
And sink in nothingness, disowning all,
If on thy brow the fadeless leaf might fall.

I.

THY wondrous tale begins ere men had braved,
Seeking thy shores, the dangers of the sea;
Ere History thy regal name had graved
A lordly race dwelt peacefully with thee.
Freedom their royal heritage and pride,
Born princes of the land they lived and died.

Ye know not whence, or when, or how they came,
Those wild, untutored, and yet noble men;
We know not by what arts they won a claim
To forest, river, mountain, dale, and glen.
Fate writes above their mounds this common lot;
That once on earth they were — but now are not.

Yet we do know of men that scorned a lie,
Of maiden courage that risked life to save;

We know that patriot fires glowed hot and high
In dusky forms no fetters could enslave.
How grand the spirits that could win such place
Amid the annals of the conquering race!

As melts the snow beneath the fervid sun,
As sink the few and weak before the strong;
As falls the hero ere the field is won,
Or stifled Right o'erpowered by mightier Wrong;
As when she finds no place on earth to dwell
Unyielding Freedom scorns to live—they fell.

No wigwams dot the plain, no echoing rock
Sends back the painted warrior's deafening shout;
No poisoned dart speeds death's benumbing shock,
And yet we may not—cannot blot them out.
From rugged mount, from river, and from bay,
Their beauteous names shall never pass away.

Defeat and failure bring no shame to those
Who choose to die as free, not live as slaves;
Honors fall on them from their very foes,
And Freedom guards, with pious trust, their graves.
Nor can the race be to oblivion hurled
That gave a Pocahontas to the world.

II.

VIRGINIA, queen and princess of the States,
The friend of freedom, and oppression's foe;
Virginia, on whose footsteps Honor waits,
Virginia, great alike in wealth and woe.
What splendors, like a halo, round thee gleam,
What grandeur dwells within thy very name!

As surely wast thou born to rule and sway
As she whose proud and queenly Dame thou bearest;
As bright, and purer too than hers, to-day,
The stainless crown, the peerless star thou wearest.

O'er willing hearts thou rulest in thy might,
Thy mandates reason, and thy sceptre right.

As loving lord bends on his gray-haired wife,
A fonder glance than on the maid he wooed,
Deeming the tried companion of his life,
Because so proved, more beautiful and good —
Even so, though worn and hoary thou mayst be,
The more we love, and prize, and honor thee.

As children over books of fairy lore
Turn with an eager, charmed, and wondering gaze,
So we entranced still fondly linger o'er
Romantic tales of fair colonial days.
Days of such pomp, magnificence, and show,
They seem to us a thousand years ago.

As some strange tale another age might claim,
We read of thy firm constancy and zeal
For exiled, wandering King, that graved thy name
With prouder ones on England's royal seal.
O days, on which a lingering glow is shed,
As smile on lips whose warm life-breath hath fled!

III.

AS blooming, cultured fields and woodlands wild,
And mountain glens, and untilled acres are,
In loving wisdom, meted out to child
By o'erseeing and paternal care;
So year by year thy broad degrees of land
Were portioned out with princely heart and hand.

Grand, generous Mother of the States thou art,
Of thy domain, self-sacrificing shorn;
Thy narrowed limits prove how huge thy heart,
Their greatness what thou might'st have kept and
    worn.

Their honors are as stars that gem thy crown,
Their mightiness a reflex of thine own.
If thou, to-day, couldst rule as monarch o'er
What in free largess thou hast given away,
Again as in the fairer days of yore,

Like wind the trees, mightst thou the nation sway.
Again might every nerve and sinew brace,
And guide and leader take thine ancient place.
The Present with its boasted progress scouts
And scoffs at what is reverenced by thee;
With cold and unbelieving spirit doubts
The holy truths it looks too low to see.
But there was wisdom in thy stern, old school,
And glory in the land when thou hadst rule.

IV.

FOREMOST in every just and righteous cause
For honor, freedom, truth, and native land,
Heedless of worldly censure or applause,
If at the bar of right thou didst but stand;
In every peril, every need, and hour,
Thou wast, thyself, a great, strong, moving power.

America had never strife to wage,
But thou didst fully, nobly bear thy part;
Had never burden of her youth or age,
But thou didst share with true and patient heart.
And hadst through all a mighty pen to write,
A head to counsel, and a sword to fight.

Wherever field was to be held or won,
Or hardship borne, or right to be maintained,
Or danger met, or deed of valor done,
Or counsel given, or honor, glory gained;
Where men were called to front death face to face,
On land or sea, there was thy rightful place,

Erase Virginia, and we are all
That makes our pride of history bereft;
Upon her sacrificing deeds let fall
Oblivion's curtain, and a blank is left—
A blank that lowers each bead in honest shame,
A blank of thought, of action, and of name,

If negligent of gain, she, wiser, threw
Her vision o'er another, higher range;
And if, distrustful of the untried new,
Was long to choose, and slow in heart to change;
She to the known was ever firm and sure,
And kept through all her bright escutcheon pure!

V.

THE memory of her fair and princely days
Is as a treasure hid, a joy untold;
Her history, fame's concentrated rays,
A heritage her sons are proud to hold.
No present ill its lustre can o'ercast,
No malice wrest from us our glorious past.

The airs that fan her hills and sweep her plains
Are haunted with the words and deeds of men,
That sounding o'er life's never-ceasing strains,
Shall ring through time, as chimes thro' sacred fame.
And, like a bright aurora, glory flames
Around her shining galaxy of names.

Go, search the annals of our country—nay,
Ransack the records of a world,—of time;
With even scales each landed action weigh,
And fins one name in any age or clime,
That universal voice declares shall be
Enrolled with Maury, Washington, and Lee,
As noble son of noble sire looks o'er,
With quickening, manly pride, the lengthened line
Of those who once his name with honor bore,—

So on each glory-lighted page where shine
Transcendent deeds, one long, fond glance we cast,
And, with unconquered hearts, *thank God we have a past!*

VI.

IN darkest hour of terror and alarm,
When North and South stood face to face in strife,
And, saddest of all sights, a brother's arm
Was lifted up to take a brother's life:
When Peace with sighs forsook the Western strand,
Arid every evil passion swept the land;
Then she, as one whom thought of death elates,
Not rash, but weighing well the cost, arose,
And calmly stood before her sister States,
With her own form to shield them from the blows.
With self-forgetting heart, and dauntless crest,
She stood, and to the foe laid bare her breast.

When Fairfax green was stained with crimson gore,
As in proud silence her first martyr fell,
There rang, and echoed back from shore to shore,
From hill to hill, a loud and fearful knell—
A knell to many it strong, invading foe,
As death cried out for death, and blow for blow.

For with that fall the seated rulers shook;
A slumbering land from apathy awoke;
The timid and the wavering courage took,
And arms were nerved for an avenging stroke,
And bands were sworn never in peace to rest,
Till blood washed out the blood that stained the
    Southern crest!

VII.

YET even then lips that were hot and young,
And all impatient of the wise delay,
At her the bitter taunt in mockery flung,

At her—unwont to linger in dismay;
Aye, dared to scoff and jeer at her, who ne'er
From death or danger shrank, or quailed with fear.
Because with prophet eyes that saw the worst,
Her generous heart turned from the deadly strife,
Reluctant that her hand should be the first
To take, though in defence, a brother's life;
And loving peace, would fain have tried the word
Of right and reason ere she drew the sword.

But well could she fling back the cruel scorn
When, freely dripping from her every pore,
Ran drops of agony, that swathed her torn
And mutilated form with streams of gore;
When first in field, and last to leave the strife,
She, having risked, lost all but name and life.

May direst woe attend the recreant heart
That from our mother State can turn away;
May utter blindness seize the eyes that dart
Their cold, hard glances on her, day by day;
Eternal silence close the lips that dare
To tarnish, with a breath, her name, her honor fair.

VIII.

MEN, within whose youthful veins the blood
Of sainted heroes flows,—strong men, who fill
The places where the dead once bravely stood,—
Arise, and as with conscious power ye thrill,
Your noble heritage and birthright claim,
Your very names belong to history and fame!

Leave to the North her traffic and her trade,
And to the powerful West her ore and grain;
Let California have her gold unweighed,
And Texas all her wealth of coast and plain;
But cling and hold with patience that can wait,
And love that never tires to your old State!

Guard ye her honor well, keep fair her name,
Her customs cherish, and her rights maintain;
Give her what she from all may justly claim—
The love of heart, the work of hand and brain.
Sons of the great, the noble, and the true,
Sons of her dead! Virginia looks to you.

Say not she is deserted—that she stands
Shackled and manacled. Let her but cry
Aloud to-day, and thrice ten thousand hands
Would strike for her, ten thousand hearts would die;
Preferring, like their fathers, death with her
To all that life, that wealth could give elsewhere.

For still the hearts that reverence her dead
With noble, emulating zeal are filled;
And still young feet in Honor's pathway tread,
And still in memory ring the words that thrilled
The spirit of her martyred son who stood
Upon her threshold and poured out his blood.

"State of my heart, my home, my birth! Thou who
Hast nurtured me with more than parent's care,
I bring thee all that from a child is due,
Indissolubly bound thy fate to share;
Resolved by thee to stand till life is o'er,
On thee repose when time shall be no more,

"No conflict canst thou wage, no peril know,
But shall my conflict and my peril be;
Thou canst not into ruin sink so low
But in that ruin I will fall with thee;
Mourning not that for thee I cease to live,
But that one life is all I have to give!"*

—*Fannie H. Marr*

*As for myself, whether in a representative capacity or as a private citizen, my fortunes are indissolubly connected with Virginia, the land of my birth, and by whom I have been nurtured with more than a parent's care, and on whose bosom I shall repose when time with me shall be no more. "She shall know no peril but that it shall be my peril, no conflict but that it shall be my conflict, and there is no abyss of ruin to which she may sink, so low, but that I shall share her fall."

—Address of Captain John Q. Marr to the Voters of Fauquier County, Virginia, January 18th, 1861.

The Captive

From *Heart-Life in Song* (1883)

TO the world of action, light and sound,

    Of happiness and mirth. A tiny sunbeam daily came

From its home of joy and bliss; And stole, as a living
thing, to his side,

And fell on his cheek like a kiss.

He watched and watched it fall

Down through the rusty grate;
He saw it climbing o'er the wall,

And o'er his fettered feet.
It sweetly spoke of bright green fields,

Of trees, and cool, clear stream;
It said there was light and hope on earth, —

Aye, light and hope for him.
Was he forgotten? No;

Fond eyes had long been dim;
True hearts had shared his every throe,

And lips had prayed for him.
But Evil can rule with iron hand,

And Hatred is bitter and strong; And what is the
might of a woman's love

Against the power of Wrong?

The captive raised his eye

To greet his sunny friend,
And breathed for it the latest sigh

His weary soul might send.
It came at last; and his eye grew bright

Watching its noiseless tread;
But when it reached the pallid cheek,

It lighted the face of the dead!

*****

Weep not for him who lieth

On fields where fame is won;
But weep for him who dieth

A thousand deaths in one.
Aye, weep for him that languisheth

Where hope may never come:
Who, drop by drop, gives up his life

For liberty and home.

—*Fannie H. Marr*

The South

From *Heart-Life in Song* (1883)

WE loved her when she sat queen among nations,
A crown of glory on her radiant brow;
Rich with the incense of world-adulations,

And strong in powers that right and truth endow.

When o'er her blooming plains and shining waters
   Plenty and Wealth swept on with even tide;

When noble-hearted sons and beauteous daughters
Made glad her thousand homes of joy and pride:

When the Past gave no echoing sound of sorrow,
The happy Present banished care away;

And the wished Future was the glad To-morrow,
That lengthened and intensified To-day.

But more, far more, when with just indignation,
At but the thought of cherished rights o'erthrown,

She rose against a vaunting usurpation,

And dared assert, and dared to claim, her own:

When to the holy God of heaven appealing,

She bared her breast to meet a murdering sword,

And with life-blood her words and actions sealing,
   Lost all she prized and sought, gained all she feared.

Yet more we love her as in desolation

She mourns her name, her rights, her children gone,
    And breathes but one wild wail of lamentation,

Whose depth of agony might move a stone.

As the fond mother, who, when health is flowing
In red, rich streams, but little heeds her child,

Finds warmer love and stronger feeling glowing,
If suffering blight where late enjoyment smiled,—

So with hearts throbbing with a tenderer yearning,
We gaze upon our prostrate, stricken land;

And with a deeper, wilder passion burning,
Sad, tireless watchers at her side we stand.

Dearer her quivering form all scarr'd and gory,
And faint with strife against a world of foes;

Dearer a thousand times her touching story
Of unexampled sufferings, deeds, and woes.

And we are learning, like the hope-forsaken,
To speak of her, our loved, our prized, our own,

Softly, as names of those whom death has taken,
Are only breathed with low and reverent tone.

—Fannie H. Marr

The Blended Flags

From *The Blended Flags* (1898)

UP with the Stars
    Of the flag divine,
Let them proudly float
    Where their sisters shine,
Over land and the sea,
    Our flag of the free.

Separated by wars,
    The North and the South,
United by scars
    At the cannon's mouth.
Blend the Stripes and the Bars,
    And count over the Stars.

—*Mrs. Maie Dove Day*

War

From *The Blended Flags* (1898)

"Give peace in our time, Oh, Lord." — *Prayer-book*

THERE never was a lovelier sound
To greet the ear, the world around,
Than the bugle note on the morning air,
With the banner floating proudly there;
The lust of the eye and the pride of life
Awakens at call to herald a strife,
For ever was braver sight to see,
Than the march to the front at War's decree;
Those manly forms with their martial grace,
And the resolute look of the soldier's face.

—*Mrs. Maie Dove Day*

Richmond: Her Glory and Her Graves

From Echoes from the Cannon (1899)

Patriae infelici et Memoriae Mortuorum fidelis.
PART FIRST.
UPON her rock-girt hills she stood,
The City of the brave and good,
Virginia's boast and pride:—
God's sunshine on her brightly smiled,
As Fortune on some favored child,
Whom Heaven no gift denied.

The morning light around her shone
In roseate hues like Glory's own—

The Day a splendor wore,
That over Rome's imperial towers,
Or Babylon's enchanted bowers,

It never threw before.

Sweet Night embraced her, like a friend,
Who would the quiet pillow tend

And dreams of rapture share,—
While from the far off midnight skies,
The stars looked down with sentry eyes

Upon the slumberer fair.

And side by side in solemn strength,
As the swift years rolled on, at length

A rival City grew,—
A rival in whose still embrace,
Lay the calm brow and marble face,

The gentle and the true.

Here twilight shadows, soft and gray,
Stole through the muffled paths alway,

With tender, noiseless tread —
And the sweet moonbeams kissed the ground
Of Hollywood, with awe profound,

As we would kiss the dead.

But Richmond, in her living pride,
Looked on this rival by her side

With only tenderness;
For in that rival's bosom deep
Her lost ones found the tranquil sleep

That weary eyelids bless.

—Cornelia Jordan

A Voice from the Ground

From *Echoes from the Cannon* (1899)

Soldiers' Cemetery, Lynchburg, Va., May 9ᵗʰ, 1885.

FORGET us not, us who are lying here
In slumber deep and dismal, darkness drear,
The while your busy footsteps onward pass
Above us through the tangled, waving grass
That hides us low; pause near the lonely spot,
And in your joy of life forget us not.

Forget us not who once were glad as you
'Mid the bright sunshine and glistening dew,
Walking abroad, loving the teeming earth,
With all its glow of beauty, sounds of mirth,
Till, for your sakes, and with no slavish fear,
We met the direful fate that laid us here.
Forget us not—we do not ask to be
Like haunting ghosts marring your human glee;
But as in Memory, holy things are kept
O'er which Affection's loyal tears are wept,
So in your hearts' deep hidden shrines and dear
We would be cherished who are sleeping here.

Forget us not, as side by side we lie,
Nor pass our lonely mounds unheeded by,
For though our palsied, mouldering hands uphold
No more blood-stained Banner's tattered fold,
Still through the ages while to us remain
Your loving tears, we have not died in vain.

Forget us not—but as the years roll by
Bring the sweet offerings love would ne'er deny—
The buds and blossoms of the joyous May—

And on our lonely graves your tributes lay,
And say to strangers and to children dear,—
"These did their duty who are lying here."

—Cornelia Jordan

FICTION

Chapter XVI

From *Sunnybank* (1867)

Marion Harland

AUGUST 15th. We have had a raid.

Raids have been all the fashion this summer, and we may now claim a notable place among the fashionables of the region. And ours was no such pitiful affair as was the arrival of a scouting-party last December, when a band of perhaps fifty — our brave defenders swore there were triple that number — stumbled upon the outposts of the Confederates, who had encamped over night upon the lawn.

To proceed systematically with the history of the event, let me begin with yesterday morning, when I had taken a rocking chair and a volume of Bulwer to a shaded corner at the west end of the piazza, and settled myself lazily for a quiet forenoon, and nothing in particular to do. Presently, Elinor came out with Carrie, armed with spelling and reading-books, and sat down upon the upper one of the front steps, to hear the child's daily tasks. At first, I was inclined to change my quarters. It makes me nervously ill-natured to listen to the sing-song monotone of lessons. I suppose it has the opposite effect upon the voluntary schoolmistress; for she is punctual and assiduous in the performance of this duty, or pleasure, whichever she considers it. But I was very comfortably fixed, and, if the truth be told, too indolent to move, unless it should become necessary. The day was bright and breezy. Rain had fallen during the night, accompanied by sharp lightning and loud thunder, and the atmosphere was the better for the excitement. I often experience a kindred change myself after I have had a rousing, wholesome "sensation." The lawn was an expanse of emerald velvet, bespangled, where the tree-shadows still rested, with diamonds; the creeping roses and clematis upon the trellis at either end of the long porch, and trailing along the eaves, were full of blossoms; and every breath from the garden was aromatic with newly distilled essences from the flower-beds. I did not open my book for a while, but inhaled the perfumes, gazed out from my bower upon the green hills, upon fields of tall corn tossing tasselled heads in the sunshine, the grand old woods to the right, and upon the left the swift river, that had caught the spirit of universal jubilation.

There are two large acacia trees at opposite corners of the house, and the murmur of bees and humming-birds in their branches fairly drowned the sing-song I had dreaded. I amused myself by watching the coquetting of the happy creatures among the feathery foliage, chasing one another in and out, above and below the tufts of flowers, that resemble nothing else so much as they do the whitest and clearest "of spun glass tipped with pink," — a matutinal quadrille, in the airy mazes of which the revellers appeared like so many living emeralds and opals. I mused, idly and pleasantly, over old tales of genii and elfin balls, and then of Eastern fables and songs, mingling diamonds, rubies, and acacias in sweet, bewildering confusion that suited my taste well upon this ripe August day.

"Our rocks are bare, but smiling there
The Acacia waves her yellow hair," — I
repeated, dreamily.

"Elinor, why does Moore call it 'yellow hair?' It is silvery, — more like Burns' 'lassie wi' the lint-white locks?"

She raised her eyes gravely to me, then glanced

at the tree. A look, part pain, part surprise, flitted over her features. I had not remembered until I saw this that the song from which I had quoted was one she used to be fond of singing with Wilton. But I cannot be forever upon my guard against reviving these tender souvenirs.

"There is a species of acacia that has yellow blossoms," she rejoined, quietly; and her eyes went down again to the book in Carrie's lap.

I fell to studying her instead of the humming-birds and butterflies after that. She wears white this summer weather, morning, noon, and night. On this morning, she had on a white muslin with full waist and sleeves, a crimson belt, and, at her throat, a red rose-bud. It is one of her affectations, to consult neatness and becomingness in her attire, to please her father's taste. No other white man, under sixty, ever comes near the plantation now, unless it be a foraging party of rough Confederates, or ruder Yankee scouts. But the artful minx's brown locks were put up decorously, and her draperies smooth and pure as if she had arrayed herself for a ball. I suspect that she is never free from the hope that her lover may appear, unheralded, at her side some fine day, brave and gay in his Lieutenant's livery. She has read enough novels to incite her to dream of such a *denouement*. All her care and circumspection, however, cannot conceal the marks of mental anguish she has undergone this summer. Her eyes are larger than ever, because her face has grown thinner; her lip has lost its spirited curve, and there is, instead, the tiniest imaginable droop of the corners; and she never sings now. I hated to hear her caroling, senselessly and ceaselessly, from top to bottom of the house; yet the place is unnaturally still without her voice. I asked her to sing a favorite aria for me the other night. She hesitated, stammered, then made the attempt, fluttered feebly through a few bars, and broke down lamentably. She suffers intensely — there can be no doubt of that — as much as it is in her puny, undeveloped nature to suffer. Well, let her: the law of compensation ordains that this shall be so. Shall my teeth be forever on edge from the sour grapes which my forefathers have eaten, and all the sweet be given her?

While these thoughts, and others like them, were passing through my brain, a negro, mounted upon a bare-backed mule, came tearing down the avenue, and dashed around the houseyard toward the servants' quarters.

"Sister, that was Albert!" exclaimed Carrie. "What do you think is the matter?"

"I do not know, dear. Probably he forgot something when he went to work this morning. Well, Susan, what is it?"

A colored girl had run out to us from the hall, in complexion the color of ashes, her teeth chattering, and eyeballs protruding with terror.

"De Yankees is coram', Miss Elinor, — de whole army!"

"You are a deceitful creature," I said, coolly. "In your heart, you are delighted. You had better go to work and pack up your best clothes, and whatever you like of Miss Elinor's and mine, so that you can be off with your deliverers and friends at the earliest possible moment."

"Agatha," said Elinor, rebukingly, "you should not say such things to a good, faithful girl. There is no cause of alarm, Susan. Where is your master?"

He was nearer at hand than we had supposed. As his daughter spoke, he stepped out upon the porch.

"I have questioned Albert," he said, with no appearance of disquietude. "From his statement, I think that a large body of cavalry must be bearing down upon us from the river road. As you say, Elinor, there appears to be no occasion for fear. It is doubtful whether we have a nearer view of them than we shall get as they march by the upper gate. I apprehend nothing from the approach of disciplined troops, if their officers are with them, as must be the case with these. Albert tells me that Will, at the first alarm, ordered the horses to be taken from the ploughs and wagons, and sent them off to the maple swamp. It was a prudent step; but I do not know that the precaution was needful."

Pretty soon, the head of the dark-blue column became visible at the top of the rising ground toward the river. At this point, the highway forks into two roads, one leading past the gate, which is the outermost entrance to the plantation; the other diverging toward the village and railroad depot. Our suspense did not last long. Within ten minutes after we had our first glimpse of them, the avenue was filled with mounted men, riding at a slow trot in the direction of the house. Elinor and I had left the piazza, as it became evident that we were to be favored with a visit, and joined Mrs. Lacy at the parlor window. None of us offered any remark upon the scene before us; but the thoughts of all must have been busy. The quaint homestead with its aspect of peaceful comfort, the well-kept grounds, fine trees and rich fields surrounding it, appeared to win the admiring or covetous regards of the foremost of the troop, judging from their gestures and so much of their faces as we could see beneath their caps and above their beards. Next the vanguard was borne a broad, gay, flaunting Yankee flag—a sight that gave a strange thrill to those who had not seen one thus boldly displayed in many months. The double-leaved gate of the yard stood open, and the leaders of the line rode straight through it up to the steps where Mr. Lacy was yet standing. He bowed in reply to the slight salute of the principal officer—a Colonel—who, without offering to alight, made his business known. He wanted food for man and beast; was willing to pay a reasonable price for what his men ate, if Mr. Lacy would accept it,—if not, they *must* have the food. The men and horses were hungry, and they had a long march before them.

I could see that the manner, even more than the terms, of the proposal irked Milord. He made answer, that he had not the power to prevent them from appropriating the contents of his storehouses and barns to their use, if they were disposed to do this, but that it was impossible for these to satisfy the wants of so large a force. There must have been three or four hundred of them.

"Very well," was the response; "we can make it go as far as it will."

He threw his leg over the pommel as he spoke, and dismounted slowly; stamped his boots upon the gravel walk to rid his feet of the numbness caused by long riding, and walked stiffly up the steps, followed by his staff.

"Yon are a Union man, I have been told?" he said, addressing the master of the house.

"I am, if you mean by that one who did his utmost to prevent the secession of the Southern States from the Federal Union, and who must ever regret that separation."

"Exactly!" sneeringly. "If the appearance of your plantation speaks truly, your Unionism has been a first-rate speculation. But how did it happen that a party of National troops was fired upon last winter from behind your lawn palings, from your very windows, too, I have been told,—several wounded, and one or more left prisoners in your hands? My information is correct—is it not?"

"I had nothing to do with the attack or the repulse," answered Mr. Lacy. "A company of Confederate cavalry encamped over night upon my premises, as Federal troops had done before them. A reconnaissance was made during the night by the party you have mentioned, and a fight ensued. No man deplored the mishap more sincerely than I did."

"And the prisoners: you forwarded them dutifully to Richmond, I suppose?"

"But one Federal soldier was left behind by the

retiring party. He was mortally wounded, and died within the week, in my house."

"More likely he was starved to death in your dog-kennel," retorted the other, offensively. "We begin to understand by this time what are the tender mercies you of the chivalry show to wounded men and captives. Another question, Mr. Unionist! Have you, or have you not, two sons in the rebel army?"

"I have."

"Officers—are they not?"

"You are right."

"They entered the service with your permission?"

"They did not."

"Indeed! But you entertain them and their comrades during their furloughs? You do not forbid them your house, because they happen, unluckily, to be traitors?"

"I treat them as any other father should treat two sons who have never failed in filial duty, whatever may be their political errors."

"All very fine—entirely satisfactory! That is a neat way of saying that you give all the aid and comfort you can to the rebels, while you play loyal to keep out of our clutches. It is wonderful"—with a laugh and an oath, turning to his staff—"how many Union men we find, where the rebs have not been able to scare up one. Sly old foxes they must be, or they would have seen the inside of Castle Thunder months ago. Why, if we are to credit one half of what they say, the ordinance of Secession would not have stood the ghost of a chance, had the people been allowed to vote for it. That is your opinion—isn't it?" again to Mr. Lacy.

"You would not believe me if I were to assert it," rejoined that gentleman, with no show of temper or abatement of dignity.

Another oath, and,—"That's the truest word you've spoken yet! Well, my good Union brother, we are here for the express purpose of affording you an opportunity of proving your love for the old flag. You should be willing to spend and be spent in the service of your country. My men want a lunch, and you will please see that it is gotten ready, for they are deucedly impatient; and they have an awkward trick of helping themselves, if they are not waited upon promptly."

He drew forward my rocking-chair as he spoke, and threw his unwieldy frame into it with a force that made it creak and groan again.

He was a coarse-featured man, flashy as to uniform, impudent as to bearing, and was, I more than suspected, two thirds drunk. His staff, with a single exception, imitated their chief, and sought their ease in various postures, more comfortable than graceful; some sitting upon the porch steps, others upon the railing, others still upon chairs abstracted from the hall. The honorable exception was one whom I had singled out, at sight, as the solitary gentleman of the party. He was about forty years of age — tall and fine-looking, and wore the neat dress of an army Chaplain. While the foregoing conversation was in progress, he had remained silent, although deeply interested, — his countenance showing plainly in whose behalf his sympathies were engaged. When Mr. Lacy reentered the house, he followed him, overtaking him at the parlor door.

"Allow me a single word, sir?"

Perceiving our presence, and divining from our position that we had been unseen witnesses of the scene without, he bowed, removed his cap, and directed his apology to us more than to the host.

"I can make no reasonable excuse for the gross insult offered you, Mr. Lacy! It is dastardly and infamous! The only extenuation of the conduct of my superior officer is his condition. You must have observed that he is partially intoxicated. I beg you to believe, however, that low as may be the state of morals among the subordinates of such a commander, you will not be subjected to personal violence, or your house to robbery, other than the wholesale order for provisions and forage already issued. If I could protect you from this, I would do so; but this is beyond my power. Whatever influence I have with the regiment shall be exerted to spare you further trouble."

Mr. Lacy held out his hand, which was taken as frankly.

"I believe you, sir, and thank you! I was not altogether unprepared for the treatment I have received. The few remaining Union men of the South occupy an unfortunate position in this war. Like the cloth under the shears, they are the spoil of both sides. Allow me to introduce to you the ladies of my family — Mrs. Lacy — Miss Lamar — Miss Lacy!"

The Chaplain saluted us with more ease and grace than I had expected to see in a Yankee parson; and after briefly renewing his assurances of protection, he returned to his comrades.

Another survey of the outer scene showed me the soldiery falling, pell-mell, upon the cornfields; tearing off the unripe ears for roasting, and the green fodder for their horses; thronging the barn-yard, in quest of other provender; and leaping the garden palings, in squads of twos, threes, and fours, in predatory excursions after the fresh vegetables, which were not daily luxuries in their camp life. The negro quarters had given up their population — from the blind patriarch of ninety to the latest baby — to hang around and stare at the lawless crew. A trusty band of about a dozen — headed by Uncle Will, the white-haired sachem of the ebony tribe, and Mammy Rachel, Mrs. Lacy's own maid — collected around the back porch to ask counsel of their master, as to what measures could be adopted to rescue some scanty portion of the lately bountiful produce of the plantation from the horde of blue-coated locusts. The conference was interrupted by the approach of the Chaplain, at sight of whom the discontented servants drew back sullenly. It was clear that they regarded the cordial respect with which Mr. Lacy listened to what he had to say, as unmanly conciliation of the oppressors. The Chaplain's advice was sound, nevertheless. He had been talking with the inebriated Colonel, and others of the staff, and was prepared with the draught of a proposal by which the house and all that it held should be preserved from the general ransacking. The superior was a glutton as well as a wine-bibber, and the Chaplain had his promise that, beside himself and his immediate attendants, not a soldier should enter the mansion during their stay, if a liberal meal were provided for the privileged few without loss of time.

The airs that brute gave himself, that forenoon, were ludicrous and disgusting beyond any description I can offer. When the sun got around to the porch, he retreated to the parlor, where he held his court, until dinner was announced, smoking, drinking, and talking boisterously with the choice spirits he had convened about him. Mr. Lacy had ordered us above stairs, before this invasion of the interior; but from the upper landing I had a tolerable view of all that passed below, both within and outside of the house. While the commanding officer recreated himself in the drawing-room, plunder and rollicking were the order of the hour, in lawn, orchard, meat-house, and servants' quarters. Some of the incidents which I observed from my lookout were pitiful, — more amusing. Each of the larger, or family-quarters, had a small garden and hen-house at the rear, kept, under Mr. Lacy's strict rules, in good order, and yielding, in many instances, a considerable revenue to the owners thereof, — the village offering a fair market for eggs, chickens, sweet-potatoes, ground peas (which benighted Yankees call peanuts), and the like. These petty domains the so-called deliverers of the oppressed race took especial delight in ravaging. Dusky faces grew grim, many tearful, as the necks of their pet poultry were wrung by the score, and their pigs squealed their last under the knives of the Yankee butchers.

Presently there strutted across the yard a burly Irishman, with a hoop-skirt buckled about his waist, and hitting his knees at each step, a many-colored shawl drawn over his dirty jacket, and upon his head poor Susan's best bonnet, which had been worn by herself, for the first and only time, the previous Sunday—a smart, dressy affair, purchased with a pocketful of Confederate bills—the hoardings of a whole year. At his heels hung the disconsolate mistress of the millinery, crying bitterly, and holding out the empty band-box, in vain supplication for the return of her treasure. While this pantomime was being enacted, a comrade of the gay Hibernian passed, leading his horse, with a bag of stolen oats lying across the saddle. Without the form of parley, he snatched the band-box from the girl, set it upon the ground, and filled it with oats for his horse's dinner. Susan gave a scream, and would have launched herself bodily upon her desecrated property, but the wearer of the bonnet prevented her by passing his brawny arm about her waist, retaining her in his grasp, until her shrieks drew the attention of the Chaplain. One stride from the porch brought him within speaking distance of the trio, and while the rescued girl fled to her mother's cabin, the indignant divine harangued the sulky pair of national defenders, with gestures few, but sternly expressive. His interference in other cases was prompt, and sometimes salutary; but what could one man do, let his character or position be what it might, among a gang of ruffianly soldiery, the principle of whose Colonel was, that it was not only lawful, but praiseworthy, to do the enemy's territory all the mischief practicable? The ice-house was entered, and shining blocks of the precious hoard were scattered all over the yard, leaking away their life under the August sun; the flower-borders were overrun, in the hot race for fruits and vegetables; choice peaches, and early apples, and bunches of unripe grapes, were stripped from bough and trellis in a spirit of wanton destruction that would have disgraced a pack of vicious schoolboys.

And all this while — as I kept thinking, ever and anon — the dead Yankee soldier, who had been nursed like a son of the house, slept in the family burying-ground, within hearing of the rude merriment of his former comrades, had not his ear been dulled for all time! Then I speculated amusedly, whether, in beholding this spoliation of his worldly goods, Milord did not repent him of his Union experiment. It was as if the destroying hosts of Egypt had overtaken the murmuring Israelites, just when they were whining for the leeks and onions of the goodly land of their captivity. Whatever were his private meditations, he showed the robbers an undaunted front. Whether he paced the back porch in company with the Chaplain, or passed from room to room to second his wife's orders for the entertainment of the self-invited party, or summoned a servant to perform the behest of the burly Colonel, when his roars for ice-water, mint, tobacco, and brandy sounded through the staid old hall, and awakened astonished echoes upon the oaken staircase, — everywhere, and at all seasons, his step was firm and equal; his voice calmly authoritative, as when surrounded, as of yore, by loving and obedient subjects; undisputed lord of the estate and those who dwelt thereupon. I was never partial to him, nor he to me; but his behavior upon this trying day would have done credit to a Lacedaemonian Chesterfield.

At last, dinner was served, and, as I heard from Susan, Mr. Lacy sat at the head of his table and carved for his guests well and generously, as if he had been feasting a select company of friends. The Chaplain — "the Captain," Susan insisted upon dubbing him — sat at his right hand, and, aided by two or three officers, who preserved some show of good manners, prevented the meal from degenerating into a greedy scramble for food.

"But dat Colonel! he beats all!" said Susan, her

black eyes saucer-like from the excitement of the day. "He is settin' at de foot of de table, wid a brandy bottle on each side on him, and for every mouthful he eats, he takes two drinks. He must be pretty nigh soaked through by dis time, big as he is. I hope he won't be able to set on his horse, when he starts; and as for dem two fellers what took my bonnet and band-box, there's a rope growin' somewhar for dem — sure! Low-lived white folks always was despisable in my sight, and I hates 'em wuss'n ever now! I done had 'nuff of Yankees — I has! Talk 'bout freedom! What I want wid freedom, ef I got to live long sech as *dem!*"

It was four o'clock in the afternoon before horses and men were pronounced fresh enough to proceed farther in the service of their country. Elinor and I overlooked the rabble from the upper hall window. I was busied with the inspection of some of the more distant scenes, when a low exclamation from her made me start. An orderly was leading a horse into the yard, which I recognized as Elinor's pet, Elfie — so named by Miss Morris, on account of a fancied resemblance between her and her mistress. She was a spirited creature, — not large, but elegantly formed; brown and silky of coat, perfect in gait, irreproachable as to pedigree. Elinor loved her as if she had been human, and I saw that she was deadly pale at sight of her in a stranger's custody. We leaned from the window to hear what followed. We gathered that the Colonel's horse was sick in consequence of an overfeed of green fodder, and incapable of carrying his master. The latter raged, and blustered, and swore at the stupidity of the groom, at the orderly who had witnessed the feeding, — at everything and everybody, excepting himself and his drunkenness. He had, it appeared, made a personal examination of the few animals standing in the stables — to wit, the carriage-horses, a restive colt, and Elfie, and decided the last to be the only thing worthy of bearing his illustrious corporeality.

I had not heard Mr. Lacy utter a remonstrance

against any trespass, however aggravating, until now — but he pressed forward to the spot where the tipsy brute was getting himself sufficiently steady upon his feet to mount his new steed, and accosted him. We could not catch all he said, but we gleaned the sense of his proposition, which was to furnish the Colonel with a larger and more serviceable animal, if he would relinquish the idea of taking Elfie. The offer was scouted disdainfully.

"I know a capital bit of (hic!) horseflesh when I see it, if I am a (hic! and an oath) Yankee!" said this image of his Maker. "And this is the (hic!) nicest thing I have; seen upon (hic!) hoofs for a month of Sundays. Bring her closer — can't you!"

Another volley of objurgations at the orderly, who tried to drag Elfie up to her future proprietor. The mare planted her fore-feet firmly in the turf, and pulled back — her intelligent eyes showing dislike and revolt, plainly as words could have done. Finding her obstinate, the orderly raised his heavy riding-whip, and struck her sharply upon the flank.

A stifled scream escaped Elinor.

"O, my poor pet! My gentle, loving little Elfie!" she cried; and kneeling at the window-seat, she covered her eyes with her fingers, to shut out the sight, and sobbed as if her heart were breaking.

Before she ventured another look, the entire line was in motion; the head of the train already winding into the village road, the star-spangled banner flaunting insolently beneath the giant Virginia oaks, that seemed to contemplate the pageant with solemn contempt. I think that I could go down to my grave in perfect peace of mind and heart if the only thing denied me were the boon of once again living beneath the folds of that gaudy rag. A raid or two more, and I shall become a ravenous salamander, in comparison with the most rabid of my fellow fire-eaters.

They were gone — and Mr. Lacy's voice was heard in the lower hall, — sorrowfully compassionate.

"Ida—love! Where is our poor child?"

Elinor sprang to her feet and hurried down. I peeped over the balusters at the meeting, anticipating a renewed burst of sentimental lamentation—a second edition of Sterne's jeremiade over the dead donkey. I was cheated. She went bravely up to her father—head erect, and a smile upon her face.

"You are grieving over Elfie's loss—are you not, Papa? She was a dear little thing, and I was fond of her—but in reality, she was the least useful horse upon the plantation. She could not work, and nobody ever rode her but me; and I so seldom go on horseback nowadays! You must not be distressed on my account, for I am bearing it very well. Our lives and home are spared. 'We have much to be thankful for.'"

Her father kissed her, drew the brown head to his bosom and stroked it, smiling down at her, while his lip quivered.

"You are the bravest girl living! We have had a severe ordeal to-day, dear, but the gleam of light is not wanting to the cloud. Our kind protector, the Chaplain."

At this point, old Rachel came up the stairs, and not choosing to be detected in eavesdropping by a servant, I abandoned my post of observation. I lost nothing, I fancy, beside the recital of the Chaplain's good deeds, which, after all, were but acts of common humanity, intensified into shining benevolence by contrast with the double-dyed rascality of his associates.

The sun set in purple glory, rounding off a perfect summer's day; but the serene beauty of cloud, sky, and river made more repulsive the blight, and havoc, and cheerless disorder pervading the premises. Personally, I have not been injured, nor are the sufferers from this ruthless vandalism so dearly beloved by me that I must needs be afflicted in their afflictions. But were I their bitter enemy,—and I do not say that the supposition is far-fetched,—I must have sighed over the waste left in the track of the invading host. Not a stalk of corn remained upright in the broad acres rolling down to the river's brim, and on the hill-side, upon the other hand, an extensive field of tobacco had shared the like fate—a piece of malicious mischief, done for mischief's sake, since not even a Yankee, or a Yankee's horse, can chew green tobacco. The barn-lofts yawned emptily; the meat-house had been thoroughly cleaned out; all the butter and milk carried off from the dairy; churns broken and milk-pans crushed into uselessness. The garden was cut up as by the hoofs of a herd of wild horses, and the fine orchard, on which the labor and care of many years have been expended, looked as if a tornado had swept through it.

The Lacys are remarkable people in their way, and one of these ways is a penchant for self-devotion,—the immolation of one's own likes and feelings, that the comfort and happiness of others may be secured,—provided these others are of their name and kin. They delude themselves into the belief that this is very noble—touching the sublime, indeed; but I, a dispassionate looker-on, pronounce it to be nothing better than ethereal selfishness, refined humbug, and exalted foolery. For example, when we gathered around the tea-table, in place of a decorous seriousness under the calamities that had befallen them, there was an elaborate effort after gay nonchalance, while they recounted their losses. My Lady led off.

"What was the name of that old lady—one of the heroines of 1776, who, after her farm had been visited by the British, found, hidden in a snug corner, an ancient rooster, the sole relic of her populous poultry-yard, and forthwith mounted a negro upon a horse, and sent him after the foraging party, with the fowl and her compliments, saying that they had overlooked it? Rachel tells me the oldest duck on the plantation secreted herself under her bed at the earliest onslaught upon the fowls, and did not quit her shelter until sunset. Would the plagiarism be too barefaced, if I were to dispatch Albert with it and my respects to our acquaintance, the Colonel?"

"You might try it, if you could be sure of not losing negro and horse along with the duck, by your witty experiment," said her husband. "It was a happy circumstance that the cows were sent to the far pasture, this morning, and so escaped notice."

"And that Uncle Will was so prudent as to conceal the horses," remarked Elinor, lightly; as if I had not witnessed her grief at the maltreatment of her favorite, and it cost her no pain to refer to the horse-thieving proclivities of her compatriots.

We are deeply indebted to the Chaplain for the security of the house and contents," was Mr. Lacy's next thanksgiving. "He is a noble fellow. It is a pity he is condemned to such uncongenial associations."

I deemed it time for me to have my say.

"His ministrations do not seem to have been blessed to the moral improvement of his flock. I should recommend a course of practical sermons upon the eighth and tenth commandments, profusely illustrated from life."

And, as a further contribution to the general hilarity, I supplied an embellished description of the scene of Susan and her bonnet. They all laughed, and then ensued more praises of the Chaplain. It transpired, in the course of this, that he had promised to call and spend a night here on his way back to headquarters. The main portion of the expedition will return by another route. His Reverence is no simpleton. The efforts he put forth in our behalf have elevated him to the dignity of heroship — a cheap price to pay for the honor.

Reports have been arriving all day of the doughty doings of our knights in blue. They supped and spent the night at James Kingston's. Wouldn't I like to see and hear Miss Hetty upon the event?

"They picked up everything that was loose upon the place!" said the old man, who stopped at the gate to tell the tale.

"Then Miss Hetty's teeth had no chance of escape!" I remarked, *sotto voce,* to Mrs. Lacy and Elinor; whereat they laughed, as I have never succeeded in making them do at more refined sallies.

Chapter VIII: A Study in Gray

From *Jack Horner* (1890)

Mary Spear Tiernan

LENT came early in 1863. The day after the reception, which took place about the middle of February, was Ash Wednesday. Madelaine began the penitential season with good resolutions and by going to church at dawn. Before she was out of bed, and while she was dressing, she heard the solemn, continuous tramp of feet and hoofs that was one of the features of the time. Troops were constantly on the move. It seemed to her that at whatever hour of the night she woke there was this tread of a voiceless, never ending army which followed into her dreams, so that sleeping or waking she was conscious of the presence of war.

When she let herself out of the house she saw defiling through the street an host of armed men. The gray of a winter dawn, hanging like a veil over the town, converged in a moving mass of gray coats marching on and on from a dull horizon in the west towards the sun coming slowly from a bank of clouds in the east.

"Dear fellows! How many of you will pass through Richmond again?" she thought, her eyes filling with tears. A gleam of sunshine caught the oncoming bayonets, which, flashing brightly, seemed to rebuke her sad question.

"Yes," she said, furtively wiping her eyes, "no tears; a woman's first duty is to be cheerful."

She stood on the topmost of the house-door steps and smiled a brave, gay smile. She even fluttered a corner of her handkerchief. In a moment, five hundred — well, she never knew how many — caps were raised. The whole division, or at least that portion of it under her eyes, smiled back with as quick and bright reflection as the gleaming bayonets gave the sun. Officers and men must all have been looking her way. Indeed, a Confederate soldier never failed to give a lady the tribute of a glance.

Doubtless they went on their way to fight, and she hers to pray, the better for an interchange of smiles.

The large, low room, dim with the half light of a partly subterranean chamber where early service was held, was filled with worshipers. Men, and above all, women, pray well when their loved ones stand every hour in jeopardy of battle, murder, and sudden death. Gray coats were again a feature of the scene. They bore a fair proportion to the homespun dresses of the women, and stentorian voices swelled the chorus of fullhearted amens. Chief among the gray coats, with a fine, soldierly gray head to match, and a distinguished presence ennobled by simplicity of bearing, was the General of the armies. His erect, imperturbable figure and serene countenance gave courage to many a drooping spirit.

Mrs. Key, her widow's veil thrown from off her face and wound about her ears and chin, sat far back in the chapel, but not so far that there was not some one behind her. When the Venite began, she was startled by the sound over her shoulder of a bass voice, rich, strong, and true.

"O come, let us sing unto the Lord; Let us heartily rejoice in the strength of our salvation," rolled forth in tones worthy the anthem. She loosened her veil in order to free her ears. It seemed a shame to muffle the sound of praise like that with crape. The voice was not only militant but triumphant, like a Te Deum after victory. It stirred Madelaine's soul. Everything during the war seemed to have peculiar significance for the time. The old Venite, like all immortal utterances, was fresh and apposite to-day as in the beginning when David strung his harp and praised God for deliverance from his enemies. The singer behind Madelaine seemed to realize the strong salvation of which he sang. Salvation to every Confederate heart included victory over temporal as well as spiritual enemies, with a pressing sense of the former. Mrs. Key felt encouraged and refreshed as patriot and Christian.

When service was over, the General of the armies rose from his knees with military promptness, and went home to his frugal morning meal without tarrying to talk. The congregation, knowing his habit, made an aisle through which he passed, returning with grave courtesy the salutations from lip and eye that met him on every side. Madelaine's first look had been towards him, and when she turned to see the owner of the fine voice he had disappeared.

She was nearing home when some one at her shoulder bade her a cheerful "Good-morning."

Turning, she saw Dallas, who had not been so fortunate as the General in getting away from the church door without conversation. He was looking bright and smiling, notwithstanding the conflicting emotions of the night before.

Feelings in times of high pressure, like flowers forced in artificial temperature, are of quick birth, but they yield readily to new impressions. A soldier's dreamless sleep had adjusted Dallas's mind to the fact that his new acquaintance was a widow.

"Pardon me, Mrs. Key, but you see I know you, this time."

"That was very clever of you, if you recognized the back of my bonnet," with an amused smile at his face glowing with haste in overtaking her.

"The back of your bonnet, indeed!"

Had he not caught a glimpse of her nice profile

and pretty pink ear in church? Had he not since been watching her floating black draperies as one watches the flight of a bird? "No, but you forgot last night to tell me where you lived, and if you will allow me I shall walk home with you and find out for myself."

Madelaine was a little annoyed. She liked a man very well "in his place," and this one interested her more than most, but his place was not beside a widow who is a widow indeed, on her way home from prayers early in the morning. It is a woman's place, however, to yield pleasantly to the inevitable, so she accepted the proffered escort with a smile, asking — "Did you stay late at the reception last night?"

"No, it got to be dull after you left. That is, I got tired. A party tires me more than ditching."

"How is it that you are out so early this morning, then?"

"Don't put it down to my credit, please. Nothing like the army for knocking late rising out of a fellow. I can't sleep after cock-crow. This morning, while I was dressing, I heard my sister and her children moving about at what was an unearthly hour for them, and presently a mob of boys and girls hurled themselves at my door, calling at the top of their voices, 'Uncle Hugh! Uncle Hugh! mamma says this is Ash Wednesday, and you must come down and go to church.' I couldn't resist all that moral suasion."

"I don't see why you should want to."

"I never shall again. Virtue has its rewards."

"Speaking of rewards," said Madelaine, ignoring the compliment, "I was rewarded by a seat near a fine voice. Somebody chanted gloriously." Suddenly it came to her that Dallas was the somebody. "Oh, was it you?" she asked, coloring.

Dallas laughed.

"It is clear you do not find early rising a penance as most of us do," said Madelaine.

"Penance? This looks like indulgence," adjusting his army swagger to her fine feminine step.

After a pause, he renewed the topic of the previous evening.

"You will permit me to come some day and bring your handkerchief?"

"You have anticipated me. I was about to ask you to come. We are at home on Thursdays, and my aunt, Miss Pritchard, is never so happy as when making a soldier welcome."

"Miss Pritchard? Surely I know that name. Why, she is the lady our sick and wounded fellows call the angel of the hospitals!"

"Yes, we have heard of that. My aunt thinks it is because she preaches good little sermons to them about their souls, but I believe it is because she takes them good dinners, and warm flannels for their bodies."

"I dare say you are both right. Man is a mixed quantity."

"So he is, very mixed. I shall tell my aunt what you say, and reconcile our opinions on that basis."

"I am in luck, having a prospect of making Miss Pritchard's acquaintance. Decidedly, Ash Wednesday is a feast day for me," Dallas was saying with a broad smile, when his companion stopped at her aunt's door.

Madelaine, looking up to tell him that here was her home, saw the smile fade from his lips. He became suddenly grave.

"Pardon me, Mrs. Key," he said, in a changed tone, "but do you live here?"

"Yes, at present, I am staying here with my uncle and aunt. Are you acquainted with the place?" she inquired a little curiously.

"No, oh, no, except the outside. I have passed it very often of course, but I never knew who lived here until now. Do you — Are you?"

"Yes?" said Madelaine, puzzled.

"Excuse me, but the world is a very small place, after all."

"Yes," said Madelaine again.

Chapter XXX

From *1860-1865: A Romance of the Valley* (1892)

Emma Lyon Bryan

ALL day long the ragged remnant of Early's indefatigable corps, weary, foot-sore, broken and appalled by the ever increasing numbers that were overwhelming their decimated ranks, straggled through the town where everything was confusion and excitement. Wounded and convalescent soldiers were fleeing to the mountains, citizens secreting their valuables, farmers running off their stock, and wives in a tremor of fear.

As evening drew on, a weird stillness fell upon the town broken only by a solitary cavalryman dashing through the streets announcing that the enemy was in sight, he was the rear-guard of Early's shattered division, and in a moment as it were, ere he was out of pistol range, a squad of blue coated horsemen galloped into the town with clanking spurs and glittering sabres followed by others and others, scattering through the different streets chasing the chickens and geese before them.

Martial strains of music greeted the ears of the disheartened, almost broken spirited citizens when phalanx after phalanx of solid infantry marched into the town. Houses were closed and windows barred, except those of two or three "*Union men*" who met Gen'l Sheridan to offer the hospitality of their homes.

Never had such a magnificently accoutred and

disciplined army invaded the poor worn out Valley;
like magic the surrounding farms were in a moment
dotted over with gleaming white tents, fences torn
away from fields and houses to supply the camp
fires, while the bands from every quarter wafted
upon the breeze the Star Spangled Banner and the
Bonnie Blue Flag. Irate Southern women closed their
ears to the sounds; others with angry flashing eyes
muttered "curses not loud but deep"—and some,
unable to control their emotion, burst into tears, while
the giddy ones peeped at the gorgeous display of
military power exclaiming:—"Oh, sister, come and
look—Heavens! They have not passed yet! You will
never have the chance to behold such a sight again,
our armies are but a handful in comparison—and such
fine uniforms, everything spick and span new—oh
here is the cavalry—do look—such grand horses—
ours are skeletons beside them!—Do come,—this
one must be Phil Sheridan! He is as handsome as
the charger he rides! Oh, will they never be done
coming? Thousands and thousands,—I verily believe
a hundred thousand!"

The girl addressed had thrown herself upon a
chair, weeping bitterly, but with flashing eye blazing
with hatred, arose exclaiming, "For shame, Betty, I
would not so honor the hateful Yankees, no, not if
they were as handsome as Apollo." "Oh, nonsense,
I'm not *honoring*, I am only enjoying the sight, and
as handsome as Sheridan is, did I not fear to bring
vengeance down upon the innocent, I would this
moment shoot him dead from his horse in all his glory
and pride. Oh, how I'd like to do it, but one can admire
the devil himself at a distance, provided he doesn't
know it." "But, I myself would be ashamed to know
it." "Pshaw, it doesn't hurt one—oh, what an elegant
silk flag, while ours, poor ours, is trailing in the dust
tattered and torn, our starving boys shoeless, ragged
and hatless, while these fat villains are basking in
gold and broadcloth—oh my poor country, poor dear

Early — our dear boys oh, oh, oh!" She could gaze no longer and falling at her sister's feet hid her sobbing face in the other's lap. Many and many similar scenes were enacted throughout the town in which not a shout was heard, the stillness only broken by the solid tramp of the fifty thousand magnificently accoutred and disciplined soldiers who wheeled quietly, almost without sound, into camp and as night closed in upon them had encircled the town with their gleaming city of tents illumined by bivouac fires, and not a fence was left in the suburbs to divide one yard from another.

In contradistinction to the Southerner, who always applied at the front door, the rap, rap of the irrepressible Yankee was heard in the morn at the rear of the dwellings, requesting, in that deferential manner instinctively accorded to the Southerner, "to swop coffee for *pies-an-things.*"

While many Southern women absolutely refused to traffic with them, others, as well as the negroes, set to work making "*stacks of pies*" for sale or exchange.

The order maintained by Sheridan in this great army was as perfect as human power could make it; to all who applied, a guard was assigned to prevent any outrages from the common soldier and though not a female appeared upon the streets, the bands serenaded the maidens, many of whom stuffed cotton into their ears to exclude the Yankee strains, while others exclaimed through the window blinds — "You just as well save your breath, we are not listening to your old Yankee music!"

Then partly in derision, but in perfect good humor the persistent musicians would strike up the stirring strains of Dixie.

The country people did not fare so well, for foraging parties took advantage of the distance from headquarters to pillage both barns and houses, and Rudolf on his return from the mountain found a squad in possession of his home and Dacey hobbling after them muttering — "*Pestes du diable! Demons de la terref*" with dire looks of warning at the other negroes who were questioned as to the whereabouts of the hidden silver and cattle, but Dacey suspecting both friend and foe, had upon the first invasion, hidden beneath the floor of her cabin all the most valuable articles save a few silver spoons reserved for Col. Waldston's special use, which she now had in a bag under her skirts.

When questioned, she laughed saying: – "*Mes amis,* you are *trop* tardy, you should have been here with le general Banks and Hunter, ah, tose *soldats* were in luck, tey got, let me see, te silver coffee urn, and tea service, and fruit baskets with dozens of spoons and forks and *helas!* We haf now only te pewter, will monsieur haf tose also, I will fetch tem?"

In the loft of her cabin were hidden many other things which she and Harry guarded by their cunning from all prying eyes. Thornton when questioned, "Deed Marster I 'clar to 'Mighty I dunno nothing 'bout no silver, Hetty, missus' gal, tak keer un de house things:–Hi yifc" laughing, "de black fool, she dun run away wid one o' yer ossifers who say he dun fall in lub wid her. Ha! ha! ha! who been hear of white man marry a nigger?"

So little did the negroes know of the extent of the country that they would enquire of one army for tidings of their children gone with the previous one, thinking they had only to go "Norf" to meet them and live in luxury. Rudolf and Sophy kept close within the house, leaving the foragers to their own free will, knowing by experience that any interference made matters worse, and when ordered to deliver the keys that the house might be searched, Rudolf bade Sophy, who was inclined to rebel, give them up, remarking sarcastically, "I fear *gentlemen* you will find that Banks, Fremont, Pope, Siegel and Hunter have left very little for you."

Rudolf knew that Dacey had hidden everything of value, even such contents of the library as was left after the first invasion. Col. Waldston being prominent in the government, his home had always been the main point of interest, and accident with Dacey's vigilance had only kept it from being burned during Hunter's raid—even the piano had been broken into pieces, but that night Rudolf's heart sank and courage faltered when he saw the sky reddened with the blaze of burning houses. Had he with his ever ready pistol brought this retaliation upon innocent, helpless people? Escape was now impossible, the enemy was within his home, and would Sheridan, like Hunter, take an Indian's vengeance, tie him to a tree to be riddled with bullets, for on leaving his home, he had made a detour in order to send to Gen'l Early the information that the enemy had gone into regular encampment with intention of sending only detachments farther up the valley; and riding along with the scout whom he had sought and a companion whom he had overtaken, heard behind them the clink-clank of an accoutred horse echo upon the Pike, and to their surprise perceived a Federal officer riding nonchalantly along this open road as though there were no enemies to be feared, but knowing well that where one blue coat appeared a myriad inevitably followed, and to be captured meant death in the freezing prisons of the North, they took counsel of each other and the scout being familiar with every inch of ground in the vicinity, resolved to follow his guidance and ride slowly in pretended ignorance of danger until the wood on the other side of the hill was reached where escape would be possible, or if their foes were not too many they might be able to turn upon them and relieve them of horses and much needed sabres, and, suggested Rudolf, touching the scout's ragged jacket, — redress ourselves." If they put spurs to their horses, a pistol shot from this officer might bring upon them the entire detachment which was doubtless behind the hill in the rear, for already two other blue caps had appeared above its crest hastening to join their commander. Each selecting his opponent and cooly pausing those "boys in gray" awaited the recognition of their foe. For a minute nothing was seen but the flash of pistol and gleam of Yankee sabres slashing through the air — this desperate fight was but a minute's work, for these three Confederates knew that the firing would bring a corps upon them. At the first volley only one blue coat had fallen and Rudolf sorely pressed by the officer whose sabre had just cut a curl from his head and having no cartridge left nor sabre to defend himself, reared his horse back on its haunches for protection against the sabre blows, when the scout's deadly aim threw the officer out of his saddle, their comrade had been cut in the shoulder and his opponent was racing back over the hill for reinforcement, not a second could be lost and Rudolf fled across the field to the ridge beyond, while the others, securing their wounded prisoner, the fresh horses, and much needed accoutrements of the officer, took to the woods under whose cover, they made a detour to reach the Confederate forces, and the escaped Yankee reporting an attack from a band of bushwhackers against whom a decree of summary vengeance had been fulminated, Gen'l Sheridan wreaked his revenge upon innocent women and children by burning every house within three miles of this sad catastrophe.

The next day after his return, Rudolf saw with horror the torch applied to his father's barns and stables and himself marched off a prisoner followed by the irrepressible Thornton saying, "Whar-ever Mars Dorf goes, I goes, he got-er have some body han' him his crutches."

Epilogue

If the purpose of an epilogue is to amplify what has already been said, then *Women of War* clearly needs no such addendum. The voices of these women need neither confirmation nor amplification. Their writings exhibit a vast stoicism, an admirable rigor, a wherewithal that in the 21st century, feels nearly extinct. Indeed, these writings take hold of raw experiences and convert them, provisionally, to something we might experience too.

The Civil War remains to us only in story, be that a story told through letters, poems, memoir or fiction. Indeed it is a story larger than itself, vaster and more complex the more of it we know. The authenticity of voices in this collection allows the reader to sense the anguish of the war in a way that is both relatable and real. Because personal experiences are the driving force this book achieves particularity, rather than falling into generalization.

Women of War is collaboration, completed after the fact. It is a collection of southern women's voices, of memoir, poetry and fiction that invites the reader to reconsider the Civil War from the point of view of a demographic that is not often in the limelight. Indeed these women give chronicle the churning, riotous heart of the Civil War. The fire of their remarkable loses is the fuel of this book. And it is a raging fire indeed.

An excerpt from Mrs. Roger A. Pryor's Memoir *From Reminiscences of Peace and War* (1904) demonstrates how these women made the most of their situations, how they gained a deeper understanding of human suffering and resilience, how they did so all the while helping others. Mrs. Pryor shares how, "a few drops of camphor on my handkerchief tided me over the worst. The wounded men crowded in and sat patiently waiting their turn. One fine little fellow of fifteen unrolled a handkerchief from his wrist to show me his wound. 'There's a bullet in there,' he said proudly. 'I'm going to have it cut out, and then go right back to the fight. Isn't it lucky it's my left hand?'" After that she moves on to help yet another wounded soldier.

Once the moment in the woods passes, once the eclipse is over, how do we make experience indelible so that others might know it too? Through reading of those experiences. The writings of these brave women allow us a glimpse into a time in our history we must not forget. Their stories are filled with wisdom, inventiveness and gumption.

—*Charlotte Matthews*
Crozet, Virginia

Author Biographies

Marta Lockett Avary (1857-1946) born and raised in Halifax County, was author and editor of several other books including *Dixie After the War* (1906).

Mrs. C. A. Ball (?) is thought to be the pen name of an unidentified Richmond woman.

Emma Lyon Bryan (1838-1916) was born in Richmond and lived in Harrisonburg for much of her life. A graduate of Hollins, she was also a poet and painter.

Mrs. Maie Dove Day (?) was born and lived in Virginia. *The Blended Flags* was her only book.

Mrs. Makgabet Figoot (?) is thought to be the misprinted pen name of an unidentified Virginia woman.

Marion Harland (1830-1922) was born in Amelia County and spent her childhood there before her family moved to Richmond when she was fourteen. Her many works include novels, memoirs, travel writing, and books on household management.

Cornelia Jordan (1830-1898) lived in Lynchburg. Copies of her volume *Corinth and Other Poems* (1865) were burned by federal officials who deemed the book too contrary to their Reconstruction efforts.

Mary Tucker Magill (1830-1899) was born in Jefferson County, West Virginia (a part of Virginia for the first three decades of her life) and settled in Winchester. Made destitute by the war, she supported herself with her writing, composing fiction, memoirs, historical accounts, and textbooks.

Fannie H. Marr (1835-?) lived and produced two volumes of poetry in Warrenton.

Judith W. McGuire (1812-1896) was born in Richmond and worked there as a nurse during the war.

Margaret J. Preston (1820-1897) was born in Philadelphia but moved to Lexington in her twenties when her father became president of Washington College (now Washington and Lee University). She was the author of six volumes of poetry.

Mrs. Roger A. Pryor (Sara Agnes Pryor) (1830-1912) was born and raised in Halifax County. Her five nonfiction books were all written after she was seventy years of age.

Sallie A. Brock Putnam (1831-1911) was born at Madison Court House and both authored a novel, *Kenneth, My King* (1873), and edited a collection of poetry, *The Southern Amaranth* (1869).

Susan Archer Tally was born in Hanover County and educated herself despite becoming deaf at the age of eleven. During the war she was arrested as a spy and imprisoned at Fort McHenry, Baltimore.

Mary Spear Tiernan (1836-1891) grew up in Richmond and lost both of her brothers to the war. Her other two novels are *Homoselle* (1881) and *Suzette* (1885).

Other Books by Casey Clabough

Creative Nonfiction

The Warrior's Path: Reflections Along an Ancient Route

SCHOOLED: Life Lessons of College Professor

Fiction

Confederado: A Novel of the Americas

Biography

George Garrett: A Critical Biography

Scholarly

Elements: The Novels of James Dickey

Experimentation and Versatility: The Early Novels and Short Fiction of Fred Chappell

Gayl Jones: The Language of Voice and Freedom in Her Writings

The Art of the Magic Striptease: The Literary Layers of George Garrett

Inhabiting Contemporary Southern and Appalachian Literature: Region and Place in the 21st Century